Twin Flame
Reunion

Twin Flame
Reunion

A Guide to Returning to Your Twin
Flame Path in Life
11:11

by

Coral Y. Cross

A Choose To Heal book
Published in Australia in 2021 ©

Copyright © 2020 by Coral Y. Cross

ISBN: 978-0-6452654-0-8

Disclaimer: The information in this book results from my personal journey, my own opinions and experiences through my own Twin Flame connection in life and my awakening.

If you are reading this book you therefore accept responsibility for your own life decisions. Excerpts of twin flame life experiences are true stories — only the names have been changed for privacy purposes.

This book is for informational purposes only and the author does not accept any responsibility for any liabilities resulting from the use, misuse, or lack of use of this information.

Cover: Aila Design

Cover Meaning: *The Twin Flames walk together into the sunset of their new life on the path of destiny. Their shadows fall long behind them reaching into their past. The shadows reach back to their birth and touch on their evolvement into the light.*

*This book is dedicated
to my one true twin flame for
this lifetime*

You were the First

...

*And You
Will be the Last*

~ CONTENTS ~

After the storm and
after the rain

...

You are still my Flame

Wherever you go

...

I will be with you
Forevermore

INTRODUCTION

The term 'Twin Flame' is something many people have never heard about and also many people who have heard of it are not sure what it really means. There are many examples of what people think it means. I get my information from my own 'intuitive thought receptions' ie: channelling.

I didn't even know from the beginning that I was in a 'twin flame' relationship this lifetime. Many people don't realise this. But over about the past 20 years I have advanced in my own spiritual practices and abilities. All the books I have written have been done through receiving intuitive thoughts. When I receive this information I have no idea when it will come to me so I have to try to be prepared to write down what I receive when I receive it. This is because if I don't I'm likely to forget it because they were never purely my own thoughts in the first place.

I decided to write this book when I realised I was actually in a twin flame situation myself. I started to see the signs and they were aligned with both people.

I wrote this book because it just started to flow through me. It was like automatic writing. I was guided to start. I didn't make a conscious or career related decision one day to write a book on this subject or anything like that. It just happened to me. And when I started, it continued to flow like a river of new understanding and love.

If it happened to me, it can happen to you – My True Love. You have returned to me.

Therefore my explanation of the twin flame phenomenon is purely from information received and my own experiences. Also now, by writing this book, by remembering my life, and connecting the events of my life to match up with what a twin flame is, we can now reunite. If you are a part of a twin flame relationship/pact at least one of the two people will be prompted to remember events and recognise the situation. Twin Flames are not soul mates.

Many people have heard of soul mates. Most imagine that a soul mate is always a lover or life partner in a romantic way. This is not quite always true at all. Your soul mates can be many and they will incarnate with you in your lifetimes many times over. They can be your mother, your father, your child, your lover, a friend or of course an enemy in various lifetimes. They will be in your life because of karmic responsibilities. Soul mates will be just about anyone in your life that turned up to contribute even for a short time.

Twin Flames will often be in a fiery, passionate and romantic relationship but it can manifest in other ways also. They are dedicated and part of each other.

The truth about 'twin flame' incarnations is that when we, as spirits/souls, incarnate on earth, we can choose to split into two bodies. We then only send half of our energy to each body. So with twin flames/ souls we will send the feminine half to one physical body and the masculine half is sent to another body. These two halves will be the twin flames who will always seek out the other and be a match in life.

Anything more complicated, like gender challenged incarnates, is not dealt with here in this book. That is a whole different story and can involve many different manifestations. Their challenges in life are completely different and are specific to their own incarnation.

So join with me as I take you on a journey of discovery. This journey is about you and it is about us. We will discover ourselves and our life connections and pacts. Once we discover where we came from, we can start to live our lives in alignment with our destiny.

– Coral Y. Cross

PART ONE:

The Beginning

CHAPTER 1

WHAT IS A TWIN FLAME?

So let us discuss exactly what Twin Flames/Souls really are. This is the situation whereby the one soul splits to incarnate into two different bodies on earth. This is a pact to meet up in human life because they are matched in vibration and are mirrors of each other even though they are seemingly two different humans.

A lot has been written and told about Twin Flames. I've read a lot of information out there such as on some websites that is so totally wrong. They are mistaken but they are giving advice to the world. Twin Flames are absolutely always two halves of the one soul who chose to incarnate into different bodies for the same lifetime and meet up for reasons of evolvement. So if you think you are a twin flame but your energy doesn't match then it is more than likely you are mistaking a soul mate for a twin flame.

The energies are matching but not the same. They come from the same source, the same soul. But they are not the same because half is the female energy and the other half is the male energy. Every soul has female and male energy within them because there is no such thing as a female or male soul. This only occurs in human physical life here on Earth for reasons of evolvement also. Therefore those different aspects from the one soul will show up differently in individual aspects of the joined couple. They will therefore not appear as twins with one mind which is why the 'break' can and will occur.

Not all twin flames will know they have a twin or mirror. This will be at least not necessarily at first. But generally either one or both will become aware even if it's subconsciously. Underneath their outward life they will live expecting in some way to meet that right person who is actually their twin flame. There will be signs along the way of life even though not everyone will be aware of them.

A twin flame relationship does not necessarily mean you are connected to have an ideal life together. Far from it many times. There will always be challenges and there is very often healing to be taking place. If you go through the traditional Signs like the Split and the Running there will be much to learn. There will be heaven and an ideal relationship at the end if you become aware and rejoin back together in the current lifetime you are in. This will be when you have both healed and evolved. There is invariably that ideal meeting up and then a painful break that will look like it is a final break that can't be mended. It's when you come through the pain and realise you almost lost your twin flame that the healing and rejoining takes place.

Many, many twin flame relationships appear completely lost and the break can be for many years. But time is passing by just waiting for one or both to wake up and realise. That time passing is filled with learning and challenges.

The **Twin Flame** refers to a single soul incarnating into two different bodies. These souls are then connected as one. Sometimes referred to as 'mirror souls'. They think the same and they have the same values. Even if these thoughts and values manifest differently in the two different human bodies their values will still hark back to being so similar as to actually being the same. Always it will refer to one being male and one being female.

Therefore, of course, their values will manifest outwards differently because of the different outlooks of being either male or female. But it will always be based on the same values. Their connection in life will therefore usually be romantic and fuelled by the flame of love and passion.

The truth here is that the original soul is made up of yin and yang. This is the female and the male energies. So when incarnating on Earth only half of the soul is channelled into the one human body. For the Twin Flame to manifest, the female half incarnates into a female body and the other male half incarnates into a male body. They are then joined in a union for that lifetime and clearly forevermore after they pass from this life.

Twin Flames are not really hugely common in human life. Not everyone can just assume they have a Twin Flame on Earth. You need to look back into your entire life to see if it indicates you have a twin flame here. It will be obvious if you know what to look for. Those who simply feel alone and wish for a twin flame — that will not produce that flame for you. You cannot create a twin flame relationship on the earth plane. They are pacted to this life plan before incarnating. They already exist before birth.

Not Soul Mates

Soul mates can masquerade as Twin Flames and many are fooled by that. But ... they will often turn toxic. For many twin flames, ogres enter their lives looking like angels. This they must recognise or the Twin Flame Reunion will fail. These ogres must be recognised and the connections broken to them. They are masquerading. They are karmic connections not twin flames.

Soul mates are all those who turn up in your lifetime to either larger degrees or smaller. Anyone who has any impact on your life is a soul mate you were meant to meet. Even your most powerful enemy. You can disempower any enemy by sending light and unconditional forgiveness.

Then when the dust settles the Twin Flame becomes obvious to all those who have them. Before you meet your twin flame or even a soul mate for that matter — you will feel a tugging sensation. It is more tugging than a pushing sensation and it's on a different vibrational level than the physical world. This tugging will bring you into the world of your twin flame and the first meeting is then complete. Sometimes this tugging can feel like pushing especially when you are meeting an important soul mate. You will often feel like pulling back and running away if this soul mate is about to bring chaos into your life for an important lesson. But if this is a meeting of Twin Flames you will definitely not feel like pulling back or running. You will feel a peaceful belonging and a blending. It will be a completion.

Varying Views on Twin Flames

Many have written on what their own version of a Twin Flame is. The fact is that there are various different situations for many Twin Flame incarnations. These relationships are not all the same or for the same reasons. Many do not recognise this and they write about it being a particular way that is set in stone.

Not all will go through the various steps and stages of twin flame relationships. These stages are mostly for those in romantic self healing incarnations. There are varying degrees and reasons for Twin Flames to incarnate here on Earth. Some of the other reasons for Twin Flame relationships are:

Healing of past karma/traumas

Matching flames on an Earth healing journey

Working together to bring about world changes

Connections on high spiritual levels

Beware of Searching

Do not search for a twin flame if you don't actually have one of those connections to someone in this lifetime. It will eventually destroy you to do this. There are spiritual cords that connect people to each other through earthly relationships. They remain as energies holding you back if they are not cut off when relationships end. Sometimes in relationship breakups one partner never cuts the cords and clings to a reunion but … if the one they are trying to stay with or connect with has cut the cords finally then it won't happen. Then it is NOT a twin flame connection. Please be very sure before you go down the wrong path. It's a delicate balance to know the difference. For some people one may cling even for a lifetime but they never see the truth of the damage they are causing to themselves and also most times to those around them who are close to them.

I've seen this happen firsthand in more than one instance. One person I know who never let go was eventually destroyed by her own self. She died after a long battle with alcoholism and then cancer. She had all her adult life created situations to keep the connection alive but because the other person had finished with that relationship, he had well and truly cut the cords. The person she focussed on was actually pacted to a completely different Twin Flame. She kept all the furniture and other items from their relationship for more than 36 years. She married again but it was soured by this obsession and eventually broke up even though she had met a wonderful new partner.

You definitely need to establish whether you really have a twin flame connection or a dangerous obsession that will harm you and is going nowhere.

Many people at first do not recognise that they are in a twin flame relationship especially if they first met when quite young. So it won't be a problem when I advise you not to speak freely to others about what your relationship is. Leaking this special fire and passion energy out to others who may not understand it may weaken it.

Observations on my part of human behaviours and relationships astound me so often. How they can be in a passionate and devoted relationship and just a few years or even less they suddenly appear to turn against those partners they were in a love relationship with. The truth is that — love is forever. Maybe their momentary passions were mistaken and not true. This can be the only answer to this phenomenon.

How can they be passionately in love and then there's nothing? No – actually this can't be. It is true love or it isn't. The truth is that unless you are in a Twin Flame relationship then you may probably have a few different love relationships some of which appear to die off. These are all with soul mates and exist for the learning process in life. They are not Twin Flames at all. Twin flames remain passionately in love even when parted. Even if they are not aware of it.

Life is filled with stories about ordinary people who are part of the Twin Flame incarnations. I will tell you some of these true stories within this book. They are basic but fascinating stories that follow the true path of Twin Flames. Each one is different so don't think that these special relationships all follow the same path or look the same. Although I said ordinary people, they are clearly much more than that.

Sadly, you might say, many twin flames do not meet up again after the break in their relationship. Well, not necessarily sadly because they will always be connected far into eternity. They will still meet up again — just not in this lifetime. Many will not realise they are part of a twin flame relationship. Although it would be quite rare not to recognise this because many messages and nudges are given along the way in life. Sometimes one wakes up but the other does not. The one who wakes up will always send out messages to their twin flame.

Sometimes the one who is the Runner will be the one who wakes up eventually way down the track after many years apart. By then the Chaser may have given up. But usually the one that gives up and enters a new relationship is doing it to protect themselves from emotional pain. They may simply fear to be alone. They may shy away and even pretend not to be aware of the other twin's attempts to reunite. They may reject any obvious advances to reunion. The new Chaser, who was previously the Runner, has to ignore this and have faith because if you really are twin flames it will always be inevitable that you will reunite.

Any secondary relationship could make it appear to be difficult to reunite. But it will still happen if it is decreed. When you are coming from the original same soul you cannot be parted. The Runner who becomes the Chaser can use many mystical and energy tools to recover the interest and passion of the other twin flame. I go into these methods in a later chapter. Mostly it's about re-energising past joyful memories you shared together. Bringing light and fire into these sweet memories and sending them out to your flame. It's not just about recovering their interest but about awakening them to the truth.

Never try to just barge into their current lives and push yourself forward. They will run away usually. It must occur naturally and involve the love recognition by both parties. Once you have discovered your twin flame relationship it can sometimes be very hard not to try to force a reunion. Your love and energy can be very impatient. Be assured that if you are twin flames you can have faith that the reunion will occur.

Sacred Relationships

Twin Flames are sacred relationships. We have bound ourselves to our destiny in this lifetime. We chose it. From the start, our vibrations were clearly matched because our energies came from the same soul. Once you have woken up to the pure sacredness of your Flame relationship you can no longer ignore your destiny.

Twin flames come here with an inbuilt blueprint for their journey. They are blessed and brave and have set huge challenges for themselves in this lifetime. They come to open the doors here for advancement of unconditional love and that includes the passion of love connections.

Many twin flame connections are here for their own soul's advancement, healing and karma. But others are here to activate unconditional love on a higher level for the many humans here on this planet. If you have always felt that you perhaps don't fit in here on Earth and the ways of the world are harming you then you are most probably here for a twin flame incarnation or with a wider healing impact on the world.

23

Our purpose is not to fit in but to be different and therefore send out the learning we have to give to the world. If we weren't outsiders then we would have nothing to give. I've spent most of my life not fitting in but at the same time it felt good and special to me.

You can't be impatient with sacred or holy relationships. They will evolve as they are meant to. I have at various times — particularly after my wake up time — let impatience take over me. It's all about control. Impatience can cause you to miss important signs and you may also miss that golden opening to go through to get to your Reunion.

The truth is that all incarnations here on Earth are sacred contracts. But in this book we are discussing only the Twin Flame relationships.

Sometimes It's Just A Romance

Humans can have a lot of short romances but that is not a twin flame relationship. These are soul mate encounters. They serve the purpose of karmic balancing and evolving. There can be one or two or many depending on the individual's past karma.

Many times first romances are truly forgotten. The people have moved on and they no longer even think of those past romances. That is a true indication that whatever that relationship was there for is now done and dusted. It's over now. If karma is not cleared with a soul mate a connection does not need to remain because you can encounter many such soul mates to bring about the karmic healing. You will simply move on to another soul mate relationship. This is the reason behind many people repeating what appear to be 'bad' relationships. If they don't learn from that first one then a similar kind of relationship will keep turning up in their lives. Many people question why they have repeated life situations. It is hard to learn this unless you are awake. Forgive and let go and do not harbour revenge and then these repeating relationships or life situations will stop occurring. It is only the Twin Flame relationships that can never be parted because they are the One Soul.

Even those enduring relationships and marriages that last a lifetime are not necessarily twin flames. They can still just be soul mates who found it convenient or happy to stay together that long. If you look into some of these relationships they are not even always happy or enduringly passionate.

The Reason For Suffering

It is the pact to incarnate as twin flames that brings about situations in life for the completion of the healing. The appearance of pain and suffering and the breaking of the relationship has been set as our destiny from the start.

We don't need to look back and blame anyone or even ourselves for situations that arose to cause separation and pain. It is always as it should be. It was all needed. The reasons and the experience of the healing and the joy with reunion are all in the destiny we first chose.

Remember always, the path that contains pain and suffering is the learning and the reunion is the reward.

~~~

We Both Need The

Completion

Before This Life Is Over

...

Come Home To Me Now

...

CHAPTER 2

THE TWIN FLAME SIGNS

The moment you meet your **Twin Flame** is when you feel the Earth move. It will depend on your own spiritual development at the time as to how you feel this. But long before this meeting, either one or both of you will be feeling for years that you were born to meet someone special who will complete you. You daydream and you visualise what it will be like not to live alone anymore. You imagine sharing your life with someone and seeing no problems on the horizon (even though in most cases there will be a lot of fiery problems).

In most instances there will be at least 8 stages to the Twin Flame relationship.

1. **The Yearning.** This can start any time from birth onwards. It may be hard to feel or recognise as a young child but it's still there. Your childhood is setting you up for this special relationship. At some point no matter how peaceful or contented your childhood seems there will arise somewhere deep inside the 'knowing' and the 'yearning' of

27

knowing there is someone needed for you to be complete. This should not in any way be anything desperate but a peaceful knowing. The real yearning is for yourself and not for another because you are both two parts of the one.

2. **The Glimpsing.** Sometimes as you mature towards teenage-hood you may 'glimpse' a photo, image or person who will nudge your feelings in recognising the person to come to your union. It will give you feelings of recognition that you will barely understand. But at the same time it will give you feelings of belonging, love and support. You may even have a real life contact with your twin flame briefly. You may also have a 'picture' in your subconscious mind of how this person looks. You will definitely recognise this person at your first meeting even if you are not aware of that recognition on the conscious level. Another key to this meeting coming up is that you may go out with or meet others before you meet your twin flame. But invariably you are disappointed and it never leads on to a long term relationship.

3. **Falling into Love.** This, in most cases, will be instant. You will know right away and in a lot of cases the first meeting is electric. At the same time it is comforting and fulfilling, like coming home. The flame has been lit and in some cases will be explosive. In other cases this explosion will be internalised instead and may only break out and become free with the reunion possibly many years later after the pain of splitting.

4. **The Magic Relationship.** After your meeting, you will usually fall into a dream-state of your relationship. You will spend all your time together and having the same interests. It will seem like nothing on earth can ever shake this relationship. You may spend many years together first or marry in a very short time. It generally depends on how old you both were when you met.

5. **The Turmoil and the Split.** Somewhere down the track of this new and wonderful relationship (perhaps after long years of marriage and possible life problems) the sparkle may wear off life for one or both of you. Egos will begin to bring problems. One or both may leave the relationship emotionally to begin with. That will bring about a great rift. You may both be confused and sad and one or both may suffer psychological and physical health problems. Here is the great turmoil. It may go on for years and health problems will come into the fore. This then sets up the situation whereby one of the lovers will run away. This partner becomes The Runner. This is where we go into the next stage.

6. **The Runner and The Chaser.** During the time when the one lover has run away and left the relationship the other will become the Chaser. This one will not accept the end of the relationship so easily. Neither will recognise at first that the relationship has, on the surface, split emotionally years ago. The Chaser may be more emotionally balanced than The Runner. A

situation has now arisen that would never have been contemplated or imagined by either lover when they first met and fell deeply into the fire of passion. This can go on for years but the very obvious sign that you are **Twin Flames** is that somehow in all this mess the ties are never broken between you. The real reason behind the running partner is not to find someone new and better but to find the love that this partner imagined, within the illusions, had disappeared from the flame relationship. It was to find this inner love within both partners. The running and then the seeking is about finding this flame within yourself. Once this is completed, then the flames reunite and reignite. This is also the time when healing will be taking place on an unseen level. If you don't recognise you are in a healing phase then it can go on for a very long time. But subtly you are still healing. So you might ask and wonder why twin flames who are destined to be together eternally could possibly split apart for any length of time. Why? The why is easy. It's about healing past traumas. So, if they are eternally in love how can they be parted? Well, you might be forgiven for thinking here it's either love or hate. How can this be? Well, it can't be in a Twin Flame situation. The true opposite to 'love' is 'fear' not hate. So to bring about the split and the healing one or both will start to feel the fear. One will usually do the running. The other will more than likely be the chaser here especially at first when one runs. They may both go into other relationships and even marry again, sometimes more than once. Always seeking out someone else to complete them. But it's always the wrong person — the wrong relationship. This appears to be pushing them far apart. But these other relationships are temporary until they are both awake.

7. **The Awakening and Surrender.** There is always this awakening time in the true Twin Flame relationship. Sometimes you have to break something before you can begin to fix it or heal something else that is hidden. This is the reason for the twin flame break-up and the running partner. Something needed fixing or healing, so on the surface the relationship had to break first. There can be an extraordinarily long period of break-up in some instances. But time is an illusion. A true twin flame relationship will weather the storm and still join again when the healing is complete.

8. **The Completion and Reunion.** This can also be called joining the circle back again. This will only happen when you are both on the same vibrational level. It can be many, many years or even just months or weeks. Once you reunite you will be together eternally because you have worked through your traumas and you have healed. You will both now feel very secure in your relationship, love will abound and you will never break up again. The reunion, while being about fire and passion, will always hinge on the soul connection and the truth. You are One, afterall. Be patient in the time leading up to reunion.

Are You A Twin Flame?

Many people would like to think that they are part of a Twin Flame relationship. It is a relatively rare occurrence in this world but is far more prevalent currently than in the past. It's not something you could count up or know. Most of the time when you think you are twin flames you are actually soul mates which is completely different but still very important for personal growth.

Be very aware not to mistake the wrong person for your Twin Flame. Obviously not everyone will have a twin flame in their current lifetime. Follow the signs and remain open. Do not fixate on a person who is the wrong one. If you give yourself a chance to just be and accept, then you will see the right signs.

If you've been guided to read this book then it's highly likely you have a twin flame. Although many desperately unhappy people may also get stuck on hoping that they have a flame. They are hoping out of deep concern for meaning in their lives. Don't get led down the wrong path as the signs are clear when you focus properly.

Beware of searching for your twin flame if you don't have that connection with someone. It will eventually destroy you to do this. Many people (some I have witnessed) do this after a relationship breakdown and some have spent their lives chasing a life that doesn't exist for them. I've seen it destroy their health and they die sooner they would have without any fire left in their hearts. Sometimes one partner never cuts the cords and clings to a reunion being possible ... but ... if the one they are trying to stay with or connect to has already cut the cords then it won't happen. Then it is NOT a twin flame connection at all and never will be. It's a delicate balance to know the difference.

For some people, one may cling even for a lifetime but they never see the truth of the damage they are causing to themselves. They become bitter and can send out negative energies to the one they are clinging to because their desperation is not being reciprocated and the love has gone. Any negative energies sent out to anyone will not harm them or affect them if they are truly disconnected from the sender.

The connecting cords mentioned in this book are spiritual or energy cords that join incarnating souls to each other. They will be present before incarnation (because of past karmic connections). They can be broken when the particular relationship dies off but many times they remain until one or both previous partners deliberately cuts them. They can be cut naturally when one or both partners moves emotionally away and focusses their energies on a new life. But this only occurs if that one partner has healed their traumas, moved on and emotionally cut those cords. But sometimes if one or both previous partners are in a great deal of emotional pain then they can get someone knowledgeable to cut them or they can focus and deliberately cut these cords themselves. Cutting those cords without going through the healing just won't really work. You can't keep traumas hidden. They will always resurface later on. So true cutting of cords only occurs with healing. You have cut these cords when there is no residue of negative karma or trauma left in the relationship, at least on one side. Continuing on with resentment and anger keeps the connection but only for the person in anger. It most likely will have to be played out further in future incarnations. Even if only one person has cut the cords in a relationship then they are released from future connections.

You will also find that you cannot move on from a twin flame no matter how hard you try to. The connection will not be broken. No matter who else you have relationships with the twin flame will not disappear. How can that ever happen when you are the same soul?

You will find that you have stayed in each other's lives no matter what has occurred in life. That is a true sign you can depend on that you are twin flames.

~~~

There can be no other
Love for us

...

But this Love

...

Our Love

CHAPTER 3

THE MIRROR SOUL MEANING

Gaze deeply into the looking-glass! Find yourself within the depths of those eyes reflected back!

Twin Flames are Mirror Souls. They mirror each other but at the same time when incarnated in separate bodies they can have differing ideas and parts to their soul. Each differing part completes the other when they are joined. The mirror soul meaning is to meet your other half. The other half of your incarnated soul.

These differences can manifest as the problems and the signs that are necessary for healing trauma. They can create the problems that cause the 'break'. The break is necessary for awakening and reuniting.

The mirror reflects back the same likes and traits but also the same fears and insecurities.

Within the twin flame relationship lies the fact that your own shadows are calling on you to go deeper within yourself. Changes are imminent within this incarnation for both of you. You are seeking. Many are blinded by the physical world and the ego illusions. If you can't go beyond this and go deeper inside yourself then you may miss the Twin Flame Reunion. You may become delusional and miss the love that's there. The running/split/separation may cause you to miss the reality. There may be blaming, negativity, resentment and hurt that you cannot see beyond. You cannot see that they are illusions.

11:11

Numbers rule the universe and numerology is involved in everything. Numbers like 11:11 that you keep seeing are indicative of your twin flame portal opening up and getting closer to you. The 11:11 are mirror images of the two joining. Your spiritual guides will often speed up the amount of times you see these numbers to nudge you into the reunion and the understanding of your twin connection. Over just the past couple of years I have seen this 11:11 so many times I cannot count. Sometimes it's a few times daily. This sign helps me to stay motivated and be sure of my destiny and that the reunion is now not too far away.

The Stages and Signs reflect how you feel about yourself and your healing journey. Because your twin flame is another aspect and mirror of yourself. Even though one might be the Runner and the other the Chaser and that may reverse at some point — you are essentially running from yourself and then chasing back to find your inner healing.

If you are in another relationship that is not your twin flame you may feel more and more that this is hurting or damaging you and you want to get away. The best advice here is to recognise that your current relationship will fade away. Do not get stressed about it, argue or fight as it may make your life unbearable. Simply try to daily recognise that you need to accept what is and open up to what is coming. This other partner may sense that you are leaving soon and also be stressed and unhappy and cause friction. The best way to travel to the reunion is to be calm, accepting, be knowing and practice daily meditations.

If you remain in chaos and fear it will just be reflected back to you. The twin flame relationship is about finding unconditional love within yourself and not solely to do with romance and love between a man and woman. It manifests as this kind of human romantic love with fire and passion. There is a door to find and open, but we had the key to the door all along. Look out for 11:11 if you so far haven't noticed it showing up for you. It's a hugely important sign.

We must accept all the hurt, pain and anything we perceive as bad that happened in the past. Accept it as our entry into awakening and love. Once you realise you have to learn to love yourself first then you are open to the changes coming. Because what you are is reflected back to you.

Star-crossed Lovers

It could be said that the Twin Flames at some point become star-crossed lovers. During the time they are broken apart it can definitely be presumed that the stars conspired, not only for their original meeting, but for this essential break. You can almost 'feel' the energies pulling you apart. It seems against your will. Stuff happens and you are suddenly catapulted apart.

Even though it will seem, especially to others, that you participated in the break, it will seem to you that you were pushed along a path you had no say in. Even against your will because your will was weakened at the time.

If you feel you are part of a Twin Flame relationship and you are now at the imminent reunion time — you can look back at how things played out. You will think there was no reason for you both to be parted but that circumstances sprang up and it just happened. When one of the two souls 'runs' the other is left distraught and puzzled. Neither of the two understands what is going on at this point.

I distinctly recall when I was just about to make my first step toward Running that I felt the pull and at the last minute it went through my mind to back out.

I saw a wide gap in my life was about to open up and eat me I thought. It was true. It did nearly consume me for many years. Once I started the 'breaking' I was helpless to stop the process. I was entirely eaten up by the process and the energy level pull on my life.

I could no longer see into the mirror. But it was still there. Hidden under the unhealed traumas.

~~~

I Wonder If You Know

I Wonder If you Think About Us

...

In Our Wildest Dreams

We Are Already Together

...

PART TWO:

The Truth

Hearts Truly Tied

None Can Divide

(golden rings inscription 1968)

CHAPTER 4

A PERSONAL STORY

(Speaking Directly To My Twin Flame here)

Whenever I'm tempted to becry the years seemingly wasted that were without my true love I remind myself it was for the best and God inspired. I would never have learnt everything I did learn if that had not occurred. So much did I learn – I learnt to finally accept that the 'mistake' we made was so we could learn to go back to unconditional love, forgiveness and atonement, and heal our past traumas, in this lifetime. I hope we are both successful in this path but no matter what – I long ago left the Running period behind and that second relationship has already dissolved. This second relationship was about this other person's learning also as he has great challenges. I'm done with that now.

It's also about what we learn from being apart. We also learn to let go of everything and return to the one soul. The Flame calls us and when we hear it we cannot go against the pull back energy. The love and the passion calls us back. When we finally see it and accept it we become Love And Connection. We are pure and accepting. Our love can transform not only ourselves but those around us.

It's not purely about helping someone else at all. That is just one part of the 'destiny' path. It's mainly really about the Twin Flame relationship itself. Because by being apart and also helping other souls we are paving the path back to each other. Not only back to each other but back with a larger much more fiery passion that is pure and that which no-one at all can affect or alter.

You can't help but see the truth and reality of focussing only on 'us'. It will happen. It's my focus and my daily meditation. Any kind of backing off on your part is purely about you reacting to your fear that arose when the 'break' occurred all those years ago. You will see the way of letting go of that fear because destiny rules us all.

My twin flame is coming to me — as is supposed to occur. Now that I know this I can be calm and accepting. I don't need to worry about where my other half is. It is you. My flame is not lost and never will be.

There's a lot been said and heard about 'soul mates'. Most people have heard of this even if they don't really know much about it. Soul mates are completely different to Twin Flames.

Many people believe that a 'soul mate' is their love relationship partner but a soul mate can be anyone in your life that you have been with in various relationships in other lifetimes. It can of course also be your romantic mate as well.

I also learnt that when you meet your twin flame they absolutely 'never' disappear from your life. They are with you for forever and far into eternity. They cannot ever be lost.

For a while after my Running phase and our split I spent quite a bit of time 'forgetting' all about our connection. Looking back I can realise why this occurred. I needed to be in the forgetful stage for all the learning to exist for me. If I had not gone into the forgetful phase I would not have left and we would not have followed our planned Stages in this Flame incarnation.

Hello soul mate. Hello Twin Flame. Our flames arise from the heart of the one soul and spread to eternity while blending together with the highest 'passion' that exists. We now have the opportunity to rejoin and complete our life journey. All it takes is for both of us to become awakened.

Recognition

It's important to know and recognise that we are twin flames. I look back and I see at our meeting while still very young that we were innocents. We were incredibly naive. But we were lovers all the same. That holding in of the true fire and passion of our union was completely from being innocents.

Recognising our innocence is recognising our 'divine' angel connection. Although naive, we still had deep healing to go through. This is what we look for when searching for the truth of a twin flame relationship. This will not be the case for every twin flame situation. They vary greatly. But I now see our innocence and angel-like sacred relationship as the very foundation of what was to come later. Although we went through the pain and separation we learnt to be innocent once again.

The Rings

If ever I need confirmation that we are twin flames it is told in the story of 'The Rings'. It was our way of cementing our flame connection way back just before we married. We bought two matching gold rings and had them inscribed inside. These words were to be prophetic. The words: "Hearts Truly Tied, None Can Divide".

We lost sight of all this over the years and at some point you lost your ring while swimming in a lake. This was a major test. Somehow we continued on being blind to everything and we never replaced your ring. But I now see why that was.

Now that I am awake to our life and our pact I see it clearly. It was to be significant for our reunion. The rings were to come into play once again with our joining the circle again.

The inscription was truly a spiritual guidance. The words are true. Our hearts are truly tied and no-one on this Earth can divide us. The only dividing or splitting was divine learning that we chose for ourselves.

Our rejoining means we get a new replacement ring and inscribe it in the same way. The ring must match. *But I still have my original ring.* It was something I never let go of all these years. It was of major significance that I kept those two rings in a safe place. There is also the diamond ring. Not having your original ring that was lost simply means that we are adding to our reunion by consciously recognising the meaning of the rings. We will add to the new awakening and joining by purchasing your new matching ring with new inscription that cements what once was. This new ring being our new life. There is a parting of the ways for some and there is a new marriage in our Destiny for us. This pact cannot be broken in any way by anyone.

Sacred Identity

In everyday karmic relationships the partners relate to each other 'humanly'. These other relationships work through the ego. But our relationship was sacred from the very start. It was magic all along. We can both look back to see this. In the beginning there was never any ego power stands. Later when going through the lead-up to separation there was the appearance of those deep dark emotions to heal. We mirrored each other by going through various emotional breakdowns. But we also went through our own separately. We had no idea how to join forces to combat our own breakdowns together.

During our break I was eventually led down the spiritual learning path. The catalyst for this was the passing of my mother. It was instant that I turned to learning all about spiritual matters. I had previously not had any overt interest. I have no recollection of relating any of that to my actual life before. Suddenly I was catapulted into this new understanding of life, love and the spirit.

I have since had a number of spiritual 'events' in my life. Including 'out of body' experiences and dreams. I have been challenged by some of the things I went through and saw.

It's important that I realised when our soul split and our relationship fell apart that I for one was seeking fulfilment on the earthly level. But I only realised this many years later. I was shown fairly early on in the new relationship I ran to that it was not ideal at all but I ignored that. I had my head in the sand. I behaved in a way that was alien to me and who I was. I thought I was alone and I sought a soul whom 'appeared' also to be seeking the same thing. A lost soul who I felt drawn to for the purpose of both healing that person and myself, just turned up in my life. I was not actively seeking any person.

But what I was doing was running away from home because I had not awakened to our true twin flame relationship. I had lost sight of the truth. I had suffered chronic illness on various levels and I had lost my way as well as my identity. I could not 'see' who I was or who 'we' were.

I see now the twin flame identity of our life relationship. I see back and there is a view like looking at a slide of when we met. I know the place and the feel of it. It was instant. I smell it. I am it. There was no just slowly going into a relationship when we first met. It was on fire from the start. The only thing was that we were both young and unable to show outwardly just how much fire was inside. I feel it now when I look back. I feel the time we wasted by not allowing that flame to burn fiercely like a wild beast. This was through naivety and lack of knowledge. The fire was there but we held back letting love just smoulder quietly.

Beautiful Memories

Starting early with the memories that stay in my mind forever and ever. The day we met. My friend and I were attending typing lessons to upgrade our skills at a local Technical School. We would catch the bus straight down the main road off our residential streets. One time, it was in the evening, when we had finished our class a car pulled up with a few boys in it. Apparently my friend knew one of them from where she worked. In the back was his brother who turned out to be my flame (you). I was somehow then sitting in the back with you.

North Rd Oakleigh 1963

There was the driver, whom my friend knew, another guy, plus my flame (you) and me in the back seat. They were meant to drive us home. Which they did but this other guy (not my flame) took an interest in me. He wanted to know where I lived. I got scared and wanted to run. I ended up giving the driver the directions to a completely different street to mine and to a strange house (a fake address). I got out of the car and ran into the front garden. They drove off. Then I immediately went a few more streets over to my own house. What a lucky break – I had managed to put this other guy (I don't even remember his name), whom I was not interested in, on the wrong trail to ever visiting my house and looking me up. Back then that was my way. I couldn't just say I'm not interested.

I barely remember what came next but I know that you, my future and forever flame, found out where I lived and contacted me. Forever after that we went out together and were an item. We were meant to be. We were One then and we still are.

We used to go for walks down that main road as you lived a few suburbs away. I remember first meeting your Dad (lovely man) as we walked up your street for the first time. Your Dad was out the front gardening. I've never forgotten that scene.

These events are still in my mind like movies. I can play them whenever I like. They are in colour and everything. They touch me with joy.

We went inside and I met your mum. She was a beautiful lady and welcoming to me. We eventually met your sister while we were in the lounge room (fabulous 60s room) sitting on the floor playing records. She was instantly intimidating towards me. I felt it immediately. It was a mild setup for future intimidating interactions with her. She acted like this to everyone not just me. Her fate on Earth had already been sealed. The way her fear caused her to treat other people, and eventually also her parents.

She was the older sister and the special one in the family as it turned out. That was because she had been ill as a child and also because she was the girl. She was to cause many a family fight or struggle in the future.

At some point after my Running I would become devastated at the loss of the love of my life. Why, oh why, could I not have been more advanced and awake earlier in my life?

Well, the answer to that is that if we were already awake we wouldn't be here in our current lifetimes to work through healing our past traumas. This is about 'awakening'.

We were not even adults when we met. That was part of the magic — that simple innocence was joyful and fulfilling. We spent 5 years together dating and going places, dancing, swimming, watching the big live bands and going to the drive-ins and other movies. We then married. It was once again a magic day. We had kept from indulging in the fires of passion for that special day.

So many life pleasures lay in store for us but we didn't see the problems or the pain of life. We were blind to what life can possibly have in store. The pleasures of our relationship, the pleasures of life together, the opportunities to open up to these things — we just did not see.

Memories flood me. The two of us at the front porch of my Mum's house. We spent time there after returning from many nights out or in the kitchen. That's how we indulged our passions back then. Kissing and cuddling for a long time. So often, I see that picture in my mind and it's in full colour. It's alive. I feel those feelings and smell the perfume.

Driving to Sorrento to spend a day at the beach. Driving regularly to your parents' country town shop. We always stayed for the weekend.

The music that was us and our life — The Shadows, The Kinks and The Beatles. The first record you gave me – Cliff Richard's 'Constantly'.

Going out to live band shows. There were many of them back then. Great memories of that time and the places we went and the bands we saw and danced to dreamily.

We went ten pin bowling. There was also the photo booth at the same venue where we took crazy photos. I remember them easily but no longer have them. They got lost over the years. I don't have a lot of photos from that era. We were obviously too engrossed in our joyful life to bother taking many.

We were 'The Innocents' back then
In many ways we still are
Those Innocents deserve their forever-after time

When we were first married and living in our new house — those beautiful evenings where we would sit in the lounge room and you would brush my very long hair. Other times you would wash my hair for me in the bathroom basin. I love these memories — they are sweet and delightful. They touch my heart today. I am forever remembering our days in the sun. We can bring back the sun and it can burn forever for us. That sun will shine on our faces and shoulders and warm our hearts once again.

Then after the difficulties of our first pregnancy and the difficult birth of our first daughter — that time when she was ten months old — we went with your mum to take her for her first swimming lesson. It was very unusual in that era to take a baby to swimming lessons. She was later to be a competition swimmer.

We were matched, just like the mirror images of twin flames. We thought the same and had the same views of everything we did together. We did not argue. We loved the same activities. We both had great respect also for each other. Many years down the track I would ask myself "where, oh where, is my true love" and "why, oh why, did I run?". I had no perception back then that it was all part of the 'Twin Flame' story — the break and separation — the realisation — and the chasing and seeking back. All divinely orchestrated. Even though we both suffered much pain and illusion of loss I am very grateful for all we've now been through and how it all led us back to our more passionate reunion.

This book is You and this book is Me
It's only words
But words are what will bring you back to me

~~~

Take me beyond this world

Far from the restraints

of time, place or borders

...

Where fear does not exist

Where only our love can be

...

CHAPTER 5

OUR SEPARATION

The Separation

The separation is painful for both partners. It seemed that The Runner was leaving and had no care. But the truth is that it can be even more painful for the runner. I spent 2 years crying and emotionally upset every day. It didn't look like it but I was devastated. I also spent part of that 2 years in a serious chronic illness. This can be the most manic and chaotic time of your life. Yes, your twin flame reflects back your biggest fears.

I saw much later that I had run away because I thought or imagined that our twin flame love had dwindled and that I had been abandoned. That is the feeling I felt. Neither of us knew how to fix this situation. But it is clearly at the very root of my illnesses and my deep emotional depression I went through a few years after we first had children.

A challenging karmic life partner turned up at the time when I felt the deepest loss of you. This is still your destiny when this occurs. Accept it. Do not regret anything in the Twin Flame situation. It is all for the good of our future together.

So the opportunity to leave arose for me. It is nothing I would otherwise ever have decided on. I was swept away by the push and the pull of destiny. I felt that energy causing me to leave. I tried to back out a few times. That backing out feeling was dissolved by a force that was not within myself. It was from an outside force. I told myself I did not want this separation. It was my biggest challenge.

But once I had left, aside from the 2 years crying, I eventually accepted this as my life now. I then married someone else and I imagined my twin flame had left my life now. I had no idea then that you were my twin flame. Over the years it became clear that you were still in my life. Eventually I would realise you were forever still in my heart.

I thought, completely wrongly, that I had now found love. But in reality I had left it behind. My twin flame and I are unable to ever be separated in truth. It can't be done. The illusions took over my life during this separation. I'm very thankful I learnt much and that I then awoke.

I mistakenly thought that this second relationship I went into was real. It was an illusion like all other intrusions into our own flame relationship. It did not last long before I knew this. But I was again stuck in my own naivety and thought I could never have another split. I thought it would break me.

The only thing that ever broke me was separation from you. That separation pain went on and on for me. That separation time was also our saviour. It is now just up to us both to realise all of this. Let no-one make any judgements or decisions about us. We belong to you and me.

I Was The Runner

Yes, I was The Runner in our relationship. It is not easy to get inside the runner of a twin flame. They can be confused and saying one thing but appear to be doing the opposite. They are conflicted. They do not want to split at all but they are playing to their fears. They are in emotional chaos following on from traumas only they can know about — deep inside.

They will always love deeply their twin flame no matter what the appearances on the outside. As a runner myself I seemed to push the love away because I was letting fear run my life. Yes, with myself, I appeared to run far away and lose sight of my flame. You were always deep inside me. I hurt you — that is true. It was not the intention. But I was also already hurt by my own fears.

I had truly convinced myself that this second relationship and marriage for me was the right one. I was deluded in this. You were also. When looking back I simply cannot see who I was and why I chose to do certain actions. It is not the real me and never was. These relationships were what we had to go through to find our true selves once again. There was a lot of learning to do.

I watched over you in more recent years when you were alone, trying to start up a few relationships with truly inappropriate people. I felt the pain then. I could have called you to me but I was still not awake. Even your latest relationship was not truly real. You thought it was of course. It is destiny that you wanted to remarry but it was rejected. Now you have time and space to really look at this situation so that you can make your decision to run to me. This person I connected to after my running is not any true connection for me. There is only you. We can never be parted in truth or in spirit.

You Were The Chaser

You were never gone from me at all. I also hurt myself and family members. We seem to have swapped situations a few times. I was the original runner and you were the chaser. You disappeared for a time because you were hurt and seeking new relationships to hide in. I woke up slowly but did nothing to change the situation. I didn't realise I had the power to change everything. Then there came a long period when I could have chosen to reunite because you were alone and free then. I was not confident of your true situation, so I did nothing. I was mistaken for a long time and thought your second marriage had lasted about ten years while in fact I later found out from you it only lasted 6 months.

The Runner and the Chaser can swap anytime and even a number of times. The runner can suddenly stop running but can often find that although they wish a reunion that the chaser is now the runner. This can go on for a long time but eventually when both flames have healed some or all of their past traumas ,they will both stop running and give in to love.

Later when you had finally chosen a new partner that worked for you – I started to thaw and I actually became the chaser then. I worried that I had taken too long to chase back. I was a chaser on a low level and chose not to be obvious. After all even though we are twin flames I thought perhaps it was too late and you did not want changes again. I then started to let you know in small ways that I was awakened and ready to reunite. I don't know if you saw this.

The Awakening

How can I know the right time to rejoin my twin flame? After all we were both now with other partners. How can we both get to the point of getting to know the souls we had become during our time apart? Well, my intuitive information has come to me. I thought I could not make the physical move towards my twin flame (you) till I had finished the job I'm pacted to do with this second partner. I thought I was bound to teach this partner how to love. He is deficient in this knowledge and ability. He first must learn to love himself and then expand into loving others. For more than 25 years this has been known to me.

It has challenged me greatly and I have wavered many times sadly. It is only in recent years that I have become aware of my twin soul and that I have actually finished the job I had to do on earth with this second partner. This knowledge has given me strength I didn't know I had. It keeps me going with life. I have now finished this job, even though it seems not complete. So I can, with all my ability, send my fire energy to my twin flame for reunion.

I am not solely responsible for this second partner. If I've done my best but he has not learnt then I am finished. He has his own past connections to go back to and heal. It is only you and I that have this destiny together. No-one else can be involved. I am too much near to my twin flame reunion to get stuck in this other situation. As I've learnt very well he is not in the position to completely learn unconditional universal love. He has definitely learned a lot and so my job is now finished. I just have to come to the realisation of becoming much calmer and accepting. I am now having to work on myself but 'reunion' is almost upon me right now. I am aware of it daily.

When I am free to send out this fire energy of love to my twin flame you will feel it intensely. You will remember. You will also reciprocate and seek me out again. You will be feeling the energies I send.

We both must accept and wait for the vibrational energies to get together and make the circumstances just right for this reunion. We must not, in any way, push or stress over it, but just let it be. Everything will fall into place to allow it to be.

Stand beside me now — no matter
what anyone may say

So who can fix the way you, my twin flame, have pulled away and gone into obscurity because of the hurt? How can I let you know it's all ok now when it doesn't look like it? It's a huge job and requires a huge amount of diplomacy and sensitivity. I am totally committed now to this path.

We both have to remember who we were (to each other) and blend that with who we are now, making sure to bring the healing and everything we've learnt over the years apart. That is the only way to success in the twin flame reunion. One person can remain hurt and not heal but the other can bring about healing to both.

This has been a typical twin flame situation whereby I was the one who ran away years ago but within a few years I realised it was not right. Your reaction was to at first chase but you then retreated for years. Although you chased me for a while you soon (out of sadness and loneliness) quickly entered a new relationship. This failed. Then later a new marriage but this also failed and also caused you to retreat even further this time away from your own children.

The situation is that after years of pain and learning I decided to become the chaser and not the runner. I realised I wasted so many years. I thought I could not change anything so I remained inactive in fixing the situation during the many years I could have. During this time I was immensely sad and felt unloved. I thought I had failed. But I just needed to wake up and see the truth.

If I had realised and 'chased' all those years ago we would have reunited the flame then. The opportunity was there. I did not want to hurt any further people so I remained inactive. I also remained 'unawakened'. This turned out to be in line with our pact. If we had reunited back then I for one was not fully awake. The true fire and passion had not quite reignited within me. All I knew was that we were forever connected and that you were forever mine — as I am yours. I still remained, over all those years — lost. I was lost without you all along.

There was a time many years ago when I was not actually awake to the Twin Flame connection but I had started to stir. You would have welcomed me then. It was after that long time when you had disappeared from all our lives. Even our children's. I began to send you the pink energy of love and connection. I was doing this intentionally and making time to concentrate on what I was doing. This had nothing whatever to do with my current relationship not working because at that stage I didn't know it would later turn to far more trouble. It was purely and devotedly feelings I had for you. They were stirring up.

It was not long after I started this practice that you did turn up again in our lives. It was instigated by you but I realised that the energies I sent you had connected to you and stirred up your own feelings. I remember clearly the first time after that when we were at a concert for one of our grand children and you were there. Without showing it, I was overwhelmed. I knew then about our real connection but I didn't act on it. I felt I could not move, as if I was frozen in time back then. I still look back and wish I had acted then. I still knew nothing about your life then really. I continued on with my other life thinking all along you were connected to someone else and in a second marriage. Unknown to me then, you had already left that marriage. You just didn't actually speak about it to us or to me.

Now it is different. You have found someone to share your life with, to whom I realise you are very much grateful after many years that you spent living alone. The problem that arises now is how to reunite while we are both in these other situations? It took me a long time to realise that the missed opportunity when you were living alone for many years was in fact a extra facet of our split and reunion. We had somehow chosen to extent it and make it harder and there is much to learn from that. The fact that it doesn't seem easy I feel very much right now has inspired me to 'seek' you even stronger now. It has added more fire and passion to the reunion.

But how do I know absolutely that I am still your love of all time? Because at that first meeting we had a couple of years ago — that meeting just the two of us — you told me that you had really loved me so much. It brought tears to my eyes then. I touched your hand as you said it.

You also told me 'out of the blue' that you still hate my current partner. You still harbour this negative energy within you. That points to the obvious fact that after all these years and other relationships — you are still hurt and that's because you still love me. If that love had died away then those strong feelings of negativity towards him would have also died in you.

I just want to walk away from everything I am living right now. I want to rush there and heal that hurt in you. The real point is here that if you still think you hate this person then you still also love me as your life partner.

So many times you have cut off communication between us. For a few years after you came back into all our lives you attended many events in the family that I would be at. You appeared comfortable with this. I now know your strong emotions were still sizzling underneath. The resentment and what you thought of as hate towards the interloper. Unknown to you when we met up at these functions I had looked forward to each meeting. Although this current cutting off causes me concern, it is really in fact a good sign. It's a major sign that all that twin flame love is vibrantly alive. You cannot shake it off and neither can I.

We both ran to other relationships after that breaking time. We had on the surface broken long before I ran. It was never deep or permanent. We were both running because we thought our love had gone and we ran in fear to other people. It was all mistaken and illusory.

My second relationship seemed to be a mistake on the surface. But it was also part of the twin flame split and reunion pact. He was also a runner and running from his broken relationship. He also needs to go back and repair this former relationship. I have had only two relationships in my lifetime. My biggest mistake was that in my second one — was that it simply was not you. That was the mistake. But mistakes and pain are what we learn from. I have learnt greatly about our huge passion for each other.

You have had at least three relationships that I know of after me. That clearly must give you plenty to compare with our twin flame connection. It must be now clear to you who we are to each other.

The Return

These secondary (or even more) relationships can never be our twin flames. There are only two people who can claim that. That is us. It's not about them (our other relationships) or about how they failed us.

66

It's purely about us. It always was only about us from the very start.

So how do you actively bring about a reunion? Even a reunion that seems impossible from some viewpoints.

You have to realise and bring completely into your being that it is inevitable to reunite. If you don't manage to do that then there is the strong possibility that it may not come about till after this current lifetime.

Many things are bringing us back together. Such as: we now have twin heart wounds (from the same surgery) when our hearts were broken (on the emotional level) but also on the physical level. It's only relatively recently — in fact around the time I realised I had heart disease — that I recognised the true Twin Flame relationship. This was the catalyst for my complete awakening. I also realised that I knew on a deeper level about it all along. There were some very vital things for our relationship that I had kept alive. Items that were significant that I had kept and cherished. These items run deeply and significantly and keep our connection alive.

Now – whenever I think about 'the One' – I know I am on the reunion path. That path can never be interefered with by any outside force.

The Why

For at least six or more years before our 'split' we had diverged from our paths of being joined. The connection was temporarily broken. If we had both been 'awake' to our life paths and connection at the time it would never have occurred. But this splitting time, often called the 'Break' is destined for many Twin Flames. We cannot live in the past and remain hurt and stay in the negative state of resentment. Because the split is inevitable for most twin flame couples. It is a time for realising and eventually healing our past traumas. When the traumas are recognised and healed and all is forgiven in every direction of time and space then that is when we can reunite.

We can ask the question — is suffering necessary? Is it necessary in life and in relationships? The answer will be yes. If we do not go through suffering we can't actually develop a depth to our personality or our relationship. Suffering makes us aware of what we don't want. Suffering helps us to choose exactly what we do want our lives to be. The suffering and heartache become unnecessary when you evolve to realise you don't need it anymore.

One day it just happens. You wake up and you are in a far better and happier place. Everything is right with the world. You're now calm and there's a fire inside you once again. You see your path in front of you clearly. You feel a peace around your past and everything you've been through before. There's also a peace around where you are heading. When you've accepted your Destiny and you know it fills your heart with fire and passion — peace will surround you and fill you.

I can now honestly say that I have learnt to love you far better and fiercer than I would have if we had not gone through the break. With an inner knowing. We now both have to come to the realisation that we need to choose our destiny and that means looking at and choosing which of all our relationships we choose as genuinely 'the One'. As we are both at a later stage in life now, the choosing needs to be very, very soon. We both need to be awake right now. Any choosing that doesn't connect us back together will eternally be the wrong choosing.

So – no matter that it took so many years to come the full circle. What matters is we are there now. Joining the twin flame circle back together. What must also be recognised is that any other relationships that came in-between are inevitably broken now. They generally are not true connection relationships. That must also be recognised. If one twin flame is very hurt still and has clung to a new relationship then the cords must be broken.

As I am now the Chaser I cannot be responsible to interfere in the destiny process. I cannot push and I cannot do the breaking. It must come from a universal place, from the field, from on high. Those irrelevant relationships will just fade away. It can be helped along and supported by my own energy and thoughts. Any sign of force coming from me will be met by another force pushing back. Force always creates another force. Peaceful action and meditation will be what is required here.

Recognition of Our Flame Connection

There are a few things to consider when you meet your twin flame in life. So how do you recognise this divine connection? Well, for me I have vivid memories from that first year. I still see pictures of our first meeting. Then I also have memories of the 'scent'. This memory is also vivid. I still smell the scent of my love. I know exactly where we were and I even know the year — our first year. We were at a bowling alley. You were sitting on the chair facing the bowling and taking the scores. I was beside you and I leaned towards you. I came into contact with the side of your face and the skin of your neck. I was overwhelmed by that scent. I was even puzzled as to what it was. I now know it is the scent that attracts and binds lovers together. It was mysterious and I can't name it. But, it was a male sending out attraction to the female. I was instantly under a spell. You were probably not aware of it. But at the same time I may have been giving out my own scent to you. It is a deep and personal scent coming from within. I've never been aware of this scent on any other person in my life except for you.

The divine meeting of twin flames involves synchronicity. When you meet that person and instantly 'know', it is the time all energies on the spiritual level synchronise. This is what the feelings of magnetism and attraction are about. The bringing together on an invisible field of the two meeting and synchronising everything about them forever after that meeting. If you are in a Twin Flame pact for this lifetime then this meeting will be electrical even if you are not aware of it.

16 Was A Magic Age For Me

I met you, the love of my life, at that age. I've never stopped loving you. Yes, I did appear to stop loving you but love remained hidden always and it resurfaced at the right time when I had learned some very important lessons in life.

You and your very existence sustains me always throughout my life and many life challenges. My love has also always been with you during your life challenges.

We then spent just over 4 years together before having our first child, a girl. A total of 9 years since we met. We were, what we thought of then as complete. We went on to have three more girls. Many things occurred after that. Many stresses of bringing up children and various illnesses both in the children and myself. You were also prone to a couple of major illnesses and surgeries. I spent a whole year being in mental health stress. I was unable to function properly for that year. It came on me after my first major illness culminating in surgery. At the time we had two children — our youngest being only 18 months old. In those days you spent a week to ten days in hospital after surgery. Our youngest refused to recognise who I was for a while after my surgery.

I started to become weak, unable to even lift my arms to make a bed or clean up at all. I vomited most days and you, my husband / flame, had to many times call out home visiting doctors at night because I could not stop vomiting. They had no idea what was wrong but I saw what one doctor wrote on his notes. 'Anorexia' was what was written as a mistaken diagnosis. How wrong could he be. They were all mystified.

I now know many years later that it was post surgery trauma (a form of PTSD).

71

I went through a terrible time during those years when I would also wake in the night in terror. I couldn't understand this terror. It seemed to be a terror of living. I sometimes got up in the night and had a shower and in the bathroom I looked in the mirror and saw a terrified face. It was out of my control. I'm not sure what you, my twin flame (mate), thought of it all or whether I even said much about it to you. I'm absolutely sure you did not understand any of it at all. I only understand it myself now — in the present time. But you still supported me.

I remember thinking while showering in the middle of the night one time — that I needed you to hold me till the fear in me subsided. But somehow I was unaware of how to ask this. I can now see clearly how that terrible time contributed to our eventual (temporary) split.

I'm now sure that this was the first 'break' in our relationship even though I didn't realise it at the time. If our former closeness and connection was still in the forefront then I probably would not have felt disconnected. But at the same time it's more than possible that my disconnection from myself and life was the catalyst for our final breakup. These incidences of ill-health had set us up for our journey of life. I wish sometimes I could go back and change all that. But of course life is all about going through the dark to get to the light.

I learnt that years ago during another challenge in my life. I was climbing a mountain. Yes, that's exactly what I was doing on a health retreat. I was afraid of heights but I pushed on up that mountain. There was no track as such, just chains in some of the higher parts. I made it. But ... then when it was time to go back down I simply could not face it. Going down is worse when you are afraid of heights. That is the time that I pushed through my fears and went through it instead. I decided there was no other choice so I literally flew down that mountain looking out into the light and also looking below me. My fear vanished. I've never forgotten that lesson in life.

It wasn't just random that I decided to push through that fearful time. I decided to focus on the one thing that had been increasingly sustaining me since I started on my spiritual journey. I focused on my mentor and the light. Whenever there seems to be an obstacle, then choose to go through it and don't run away or try to avoid it. What is possible to change is the future and destiny. We chose our lives together to learn and eventually be reunited with new insight and understanding and with more powerful fire and passion. This was all in our destiny.

Remember The Real People

Yes, it is always the two real people I remember. It's not those two foolish people (who are in reality illusions) who existed during our relationship decline and split. Those two don't exist anymore. I have healed on many emotional levels since then. You have also. This is the purpose of the split and reunion. We still love those people we were as teenagers and for many years after that. We just don't relate to the two twin flame lovers who broke apart and forgot who they were. Just like at birth, we fell into forgetfulness for a while.

Pure Memories Seemed To Be Lost

I lost sight of the pure memories for a while. This was because I focussed on my current illusory pain and fear of loss.

Then a lot was covered up by chronic illness, pain and suffering. When you lose sight of your love then your body reacts and becomes ill.

It was as simple as that. I lost sight. Fear of loss can cause the appearance of actual loss. Now I've gained my insight back I have to reunite with the true love of my life.

This is You, my Twin.

~~~

CHAPTER 6

THE TURNING

The Turning

It took a few short years of trying to fix this second relationship for me to finally make the turning. I turned away when life seemed empty and I had emptied myself with the trying to fix another person. It can't be done.

I am no longer concerned with fixing this and I'm not even allowing myself to get involved in it. It's a major change — a major turn. It was always just a part of my learning. This second marriage is now so very empty. It took me a while to recognise this and see it even though it was very obvious for many years. I failed to act on it. I can now let go easily. There was never any kind of real connection there. How could there be any connection with anyone at all unless it is You?

It is a matter of truth that twin flames often choose to meet other people who are quite hard to love. This is in fact a part of our twin flame pact — these other people are in our lives so we can learn unconditional love. It's part of the twin flame incarnation and learning. It seems so cruel and unhappy and can be ongoing for many years. But that's only until we wake up and realise. We need to unconditionally love these other people and show them compassion before we can move back to our twin flame. These secondary people in our lives can push us to our limits. It's very tempting to give in to anger and resentment but these are the very energies we are to transmute into love.

It's because if our split and separation is for learning then how would we learn unless we meet other people who challenge us. Nice and loveable people are easy to love — no challenge there. We go through the hell of other relationships to learn not only the unconditional love but we also learn who our twin flame is. We learn to reunite. We also learn to speak up against the odds. This is something I could not ever do before.

I realised I had never cut the cords to you, my first love, my twin flame. I thought I had for a few years but realised we were still and forever connected just a few years after the break. I did not cut the cords because it was something I absolutely never would want to do. As twin flames it is also impossible to cut connections. With the trauma of our break I had made a kind of foolish promise to myself I would never let this second relationship break down in any way. But that's because I did not have the twin flame recognition back then when I was not awake.

'Destiny' had it's way with forcing this second breakdown simply because it was meant to be. Circumstances beyond my control led to this second split. It was guidance beyond me that caused it to help me to decide to leave without regrets.

76

I'm now just waiting on the flame igniting again. The original first flame that will now be the last flame. You were the first — you'll be the last. But all along it was an eternal flame.

This world may end but not you and I. I miss the part of you that is me. More than I can ever say. My life is so much better than I thought it could ever be because you are half of it.

No-one Can Come Between Us

Far from resenting the second marriages we entered into we must both realise that these failures were the catalyst for our 'knowing' about our reunion and connection. This was a major part of our learning. In my own case I clung onto this second relationship because I did not want anymore failed relationships or anymore breaks. I was remembering our own painful break. I was hiding from the truth. This caused me to cling for far too long.

Another relationship sprung up for you, my flame, in this period. You had desired this for many years. I failed to realise that it was your longing for us that catapulted you into a new relationship. You thought you were now 'happy'. There were signs of things about this new relationship that I could see did not satisfy you fully. It was these signs that showed me it would end and then the way was open for our reunion. My inner self cannot exist without you.

The Twin Flame connection does not allow for running into a new relationship that could ever be permanent or for trying to hide away. The connection is stronger than all of that.

While life seems to be a struggle to get through while I'm waiting for that right time — it's still essential to let go and invite the higher energies into life as it currently is. This will facilitate all the energies to come together at the right time for the reunion. If you give in and don't live through a struggle then you may just stay there and not move on and up.

You know I could have walked into your arms at any time a few years ago. But I waited and didn't see the truth. Now that opportunity that would have been easy has passed us by. But of course in the bigger picture I can see that the harder it is to get to the reunion the better it will eventually be. It will be all the sweeter. Also the more challenges we go through, the more passionate and fiery will be the reuniting. Now it means the reunion will bring about a more complete healing than if it had been easy.

I see clearly now that my second marriage failed because I had not stopped loving you, my twin flame. This seeped through into the second relationship. I never disclosed this continuing fact to anyone but it does get through on a different level. It causes a huge gap in any new relationship. This can then sour that relationship and cause awakening in the heart for the flame.

The thing you need to be aware of is that this second marriage was over years ago. It is currently lifeless. I wish I had told you this years ago but in fact I had hidden it from myself too. I remained, on the surface, thinking it was all ok when in fact it was not.

I am conflicted. Not so conflicted as to not be aware that I'm on the twin flame reunion path so I

Twin Flame Reunion

can't be wavered from that. My life currently is in a turmoil. Everything is coming together for the reunion. The lovers will be back together as it should be. But it means changing our entire lives as they are right now. I need to be brave enough and so do you.

I have many times been saddened by all the time we spent apart. But I do know how much I've learnt with this huge separation. I now absolutely 'know' we are meant for each other. Whereas that revelation may have passed me by if we had not had this split. We may both have simply lived out an ordinary life together and we may have let the passion die. Instead now we have the opportunity to fire it up and live the passion.

The new code is – I'm never going to give you up, never going to run away, or hurt you. Yes, it has already been done but it is never to be ever again. Have I ever needed you more than right now? Yes – I've needed you since before we were even born here.

Opportunity Opens Doors

Something for you to recognise here and now is the fact that you now have the open opportunity to come and get me. Come and pick me up with my bags and I'm ready to go with you to anywhere on Earth. This is what you desired after the split. You tried and I missed the signs. I wish you had known how to wake me up because I was under a spell of devastation, believing (untruly) that I had lost your love for me.

Now I'm ready — are you ready?

Ready to claim me, your true love, and take me away yourself. Just drive up in your car and take me. I will be wearing my 60s dress to suit the occasion and the car. I can never not love you and I can never ever let you down ever again in this lifetime. Let's be deliriously happy in the last and most important years of our lives.

Within my awakening came the realisation of: "the awful thought that – what if I'd never known you".

My whole life would have been worth nothing to me. I can't even imagine or bear the thought of having lived this life without you in it.

This is simply a realisation of what you are to me. It is not even possible that I could have lived this life without you — because our pact was made before we came here. But I can easily now look back and see that if you had not shown up for me in this life then it would have been worthless.

We're still the Young Ones
Young ones shouldn't be afraid
This is the time to be Brave

I still need to tell you

...

In the Living Years

While we are still here

...

You'll always be the One

81

End Blaming

Let us put an end to 'blaming'. We can stop believing past generations harmed us and we can help to heal our own next generations that we created. While we are still living on this Earth we can return to unconditional love and reunite the twin flames.

Many years ago I started to realise that you are my one and only. I practised sending you love energy and on an emotional level I called you back to me. This concurs with the time when you sent a CD to our children. What an incredible synchronising event this was. It was around the time I was sending you the pink energy to mend broken hearts. You reached out then.

Neither of us really connected these acts with my own sending of love. But it stayed in my mind forever after. It was soon after that when you turned up at that concert for our grand daughter. I was stunned by your presence that day. I wanted you in my life forevermore right then. But I still felt stuck where I was and I was very much uncertain about how you felt.

Never Judge Others

Many friends and relatives saw my running as cheating. I've always maintained that it was not cheating. Reason: Because although we were married we had not enjoyed any kind of intimate relationship for at least 6 years before I ran. I was lost and I needed my twin flame but it was not anyone's fault. Neither one of us decided against this. You didn't know how to 'be' with me and navigate our family and life problems. I see that now. I was needful emotionally. I thought I had lost my love and the very deepness of my soul cried inside. I was fully conscious of this large missing gap in our true relationship. But ... and this is the crucial thing – I was waiting. Waiting, waiting, waiting. For what? I was waiting for you to come to me with tenderness and love and complete our intimate relationship to each other without the mad world outside damaging us or stopping us.

I waited far too long. We just allowed the world outside of us to cause us harm and separation. Words would have been said in this 6 year period that we both would want to call back and eliminate. Fear causes lashing out. But on the surface it all looked fine. We continued on living a family life. Just that both of us were hurt and alone. If only we were both awake back then we would have run to each other and never let go. This scene plays out in my mind many times over.

I wanted to reach out to you many times in that period. I wanted to co-ordinate our responses to life pressures. I was desiring them to be the same but they seemed completely opposite then.

While your apparent 'hatred' of my second marriage partner seems real to you — it is a fact that this relationship did not in any way cause our split. It seemed to you at the time that someone had taken me away from you. It certainly looked like that to everyone. But ... I was unwell and unable to think properly for myself at that time.

I want you to know this.

Heart to Heart

If only we had lived 'heart-to-heart' all that time when we had drifted, and both were afraid, and fear broke us. We should have, at all times, remembered the inscription in both our gold wedding rings. 'Hearts Truly Tied, None Can Divide' and our names and wedding date. Not only that but when you were swimming in a lake around 1980, your ring was lost. It came off your finger in the water. It was a large country lake. No way to find it. Why didn't I register devastation? Why didn't we replace it with a new one? See the paragraph 'The Rings'.

This is an action that would speak of our devotion and passion. All this true devotion and passion had been pushed below the surface for us. We had started out so very young and naive. Did I myself even know what fiery passion was back then? It has smouldered in me since birth but was hidden all this time waiting to be released. Just the era in which we were both born brought us up to keep those kinds of passions under the surface — even to the degree that we could not even see them for ourselves.

But believe me they were there all along. They tried to resurface within both of us during the long break. We sought others to fill this void. It was not ever going to work with these other partners.

Now that I have awoken to the flame and destiny this fire and passion is pushing against me trying to explode out into the world and into you. You also have this passionate energy always trying to burgeon out of you. But it can never be completed until the time of our reunion.

How You Supported Me

Even so, over all the years we were together, you supported me in many crucial areas of my life. I want to Thank You for this. It's not forgotten.

No-one will ever touch me more than you

I had numerous challenges during our relationship. These were basically personal challenges. None were caused by our relationship. It started with my health. We both went through the challenge of a problem whereby we could not have children straight away. All other couples we knew were having their first children. We appeared out of place for that all those years ago. We worked on the problem together. By the time I was pregnant with our first child major problems came up for me. My entire pregnancy was filled with problems. Continuous nausea and vomiting that culminated in a day of it every ten minutes or so.

That was a fateful day for me for the future. I was given two injections of a drug I had major side effects from that would go far into my life and cause me a lot of problems. It affected my central nervous system. The problems of vomiting and also not being able to eat much continued. I was not informed at that time what this meant. I have only just in very recent times found out it was a serious condition called HG (Hyperemesis gravidarum) pregnancy. It's a rare condition affecting only 2% of pregnancies. I lost weight and consequently lost the special diamond engagement ring we purchased together back in the 60s. It simply fell off my finger while I was out in the local area shopping. Lucky it was insured. I got another one. Not the same thing, but not the first time the original ring was to be replaced as it turned out.

Later I was to get swollen hands and fingers from pregnancy and had to have my two rings cut off my finger. I kept it in a drawer in our bedroom. About a year later it was found to be gone. It had been stolen. So once again this ring was replaced.

How I Also Supported You

There were many times I needed also to support you. You also had a number of crises in our lives together. I like to think I supported you as much as you supported me. This support we remember in our background is one of the main basics of how we are connected by the Twin Flame incarnation. It binds us with love.

I recall how when pregnant with our first child you started to suffer stomach pains in the later part of the pregnancy. The doctor said they were pains some men get because they identify with the birth too much. In other words, we can see in the now, that you were easily one half of a twin flame relationship. Feeling the pain that I would go through a bit later on and identifying with me and what I would go through.

Before we even had children and had only been married a relatively short time you got very ill one day. I could not drive you to hospital but a doctor visited us and had you sent to hospital. Appendicitis they said. When you had been in hospital about a week after the surgery they found you not to be recovering right and that you had some kind of infection. They thought it was hepatitis from the surgery. So all the patients in the hospital had to be vaccinated and you were sent away to the Infectious Diseases Hospital. I think you were in hospital at that time for around 3-4 weeks. Our time apart at so young an age was very disturbing for me. I ended up going to stay at your parents' house and we would all go to visit you in hospital. It was a strain for me then and not too pleasant for you also. When you eventually came home — after that hospital telling you that you never even had hepatitis — you were still weak and painful. We had to take renewing our relationship very tenderly and carefully.

In later years you were once again to have major health problems with two separate episodes of kidney stones with more surgery and more stays in hospital. That is a very painful condition.

You also went through an unprecedented time when you suffered a retrenchment at work. This was something people of the previous era we lived through of the 60s and 70s virtually never had to contend with. You were a hard and conscientious worker. Suddenly you were thrust into a world whereby you could possibly not support your family or pay the mortgage. Our children were still young of course. You fell into a depression and a kind of panic. It was scary for me too to see you like this. Not to worry though — being such a conscientious and professional person you had another good job within two weeks.

There were also the two times since our separation that you were very ill and on death's door. I visited you both of those times. On both occasions you were so ill I doubt you remember I was even there. But I showed you concern and support when you had that major heart attack. I rushed to the hospital from work because I was frantic that you would die. It was me you asked to contact your sister. Your sister who does not like me or talk to me. You gave me her number and I contacted her to let her know of your critical condition. She was a bit put out that it was me contacting her. I no longer cared about any of that kind of animosity. You had just been in ICU and I would say you don't remember me being there holding your hand. I've been there myself after open heart surgery and I lost my memories of the time of being in ICU and just after that.

The other time it was the fluid collected around your heart and lungs. You were also very ill that time and before that you previously had a pacemaker fitted. You told me many things I had never heard before. You suddenly became very forthcoming with truths with me and it was the first time I knew your second marriage had only lasted 6 months. That was years and years ago. I was stunned by this. I thought of all the years we could have saved by being together again sooner. If I had known this fact. But not to be. I know you didn't even remember telling me all of this about your life story because when I spoke to you much later you didn't remember. It does not matter. What matters is that I was there and we connected both times. Your soul and mine knew I was there for you.

I was there for you and you were falling apart and it left a mark on my heart. Did it leave any mark on your own heart?

I Can No Longer Ignore

I can no longer ignore the memories of who we really are. I spend time each day living the good times we had. The memories of your sweetness and beauty remain with me forever. Our teenage years and the 60s were just the most beautiful times for me and I'm very sure also for you.

This is a private pact between the two of us. We can no longer not participate in the rejoining. Those two people who were in relationships with us up until our awakening must stand aside. They must not be harmed or hurt in any way but they have their own life paths to follow. For a while they were with us to participate in our challenges and our reunion.

After that they must follow their own direction. They both more than likely have other mates and relationships to go back and examine and see what they may owe to those people they left behind also.

It's an amazing privilege to have participated in this life destiny pact. I feel the joy and connection of this special pact deep within myself.

I Was Running From The Truth

I was running from the truth of us. But the thing is that I wasn't aware of it at that time. I had lost sight of who we really are and who we really were. Our forever connection wasn't visible to me through the veil of pain and chaos.

I see now how this veil gradually became more and more transparent over a number of years. That is the way of learning. It seeps in gradually to the human mind.

I could easily have turned back to you a few years ago when you first started into car clubs. But still I was not fully awake then. Still I seemed frozen.

Eventually I could see right through the veil very clearly. I was galvanised into action from then on. Without action your destiny can't be realised into fact.

I was now getting ready to move into the truth

You Were The Only One

From my earlier teenage years I met a few boys and went out with some but I didn't connect with any. None were long term relationships. I usually ran away and wasn't interested. Not till I met you.

You always were the only one for me. I also shied away from even going out with a few who sought me out. Not interested once again. So how did I know when I met you that everything was right from that moment? I just did. It was intuition about destiny.

We would go out a lot and to the beach, visit friends or relatives, dancing, music, and joy. No technology interfered and our lives were not filled with psychological problems and illness. There were no feelings of isolation whatsoever.

Now people are stuck to rectangles (phones) staring at them, so isolation and illness is rife. We lived and loved through a wonderful time.

So now if we take away the heartache (illusion) we can make our lives a heaven on Earth.

You'll always be the One

Don't Lose That Loving Feeling

Because once you do, you will become isolated from others and each other. You may also become ill. Your life no longer contains the joy of living. I have now learnt this but only from the experience of a break-up with you.

We lost it for a while years ago but it's back now with a passion and fire. That is as it must be if we are twin flames.

Every time I go down to the Peninsula I think of you. I am with you. The memories and reality of you flood me.

We must always examine our closest relationships in this life and of course particularly within a twin flame relationship. We must examine every tiny particle of what has transpired before we can reunite. When I now look at the truths from the past I see some of what I believed to be true was not at all true. We can be deceived by ourselves and our mistaken beliefs.

Always love and never forget to feel it, show it and be it. Be there always for your twin flame no matter what the appearances seem on the surface. This way you will never forget to return to the One.

People can wither away and die to the world if the loving feeling is withheld. It's the one most important feeling to keep alive in our hearts.

Think Very Carefully

Ask yourself — "who is the love of my life?". If either of us are in other relationships we must take some serious time to think it over. Are these partners sharing all of themselves with us? Are we even doing that also? Does your secondary partner put you first in every decision and also bring you gifts?

If we examine the whole situation and find that those partners are not sharing their wholeness with us then this is the test. I already have awoken to our twin flame relationship. But if you have not yet done this — realise that only twin flames share all of themselves with the other. Is there some part of the new partner that is held back? It is for certain that this would be the case. Sharing all, such as love of pets and of your own children and family. Sharing a place to live and assets is another measurement of the love and commitment.

I'm totally ready to sell everything and join with you in living in a house that is just for us. I recall in our earlier time together that we shared absolutely everything before we got off the rails and declined (only in our illusions). This is a fact everyone must consider in their relationships. This is how to allow the twin flame connection to show you the way.

Absolutely nothing about a true love relationship within the flame is about assets or money or keeping back from sharing. The ideal is — we join everything we have and run off into the sunset together for a life bathed in that beautiful sun and its warmth.

We once shared everything of ourselves and now we are to reunite we will once again share everything but even deeper with a renewed understanding. Deep within us we never stopped sharing.

The essence of who we were together originally is still there. But we have evolved and changed into the flame twins.

The couple who can now relate to each other in sacred purity. Nothing can be held back now or ever.

We cannot live our lives concentrating only on the physical and the material world that seems to help us but is in fact, only on the surface. We now need to choose our lives based on love and commitment and live with truth. This sustains us and it matters not where we live or what items or superficial people are in our lives. All that matters is that where we live, our twin flame is with us and that we live a meaningful life. That the twin flames share their passionate lives with each other. All else means absolutely nothing.

Twin Flames Are Fortunate

Just the acceptance and knowledge that we are Twin Flames brings us good fortune. It is a privilege to recognise this.

We are one and there is no going back from that. Look at me and remember. Wipe away the times when we seemed out of sync. Put together only the times when the flame was joined and work on the rest of your life with this in mind. The joy and sharing that can come about once again. We may have a relatively short time left here, so why not choose the fire of passion and completion.

Destiny

We've all heard the word destiny. This word holds a certain magnetic music to me. This word alone brings me peace and a certain kind of wonder that attracts me to it. It magnetically pulls me to it. It is our guided choice all along. It's not set in stone as many believe but it is changeable according to our free will. Also according to how fast we evolve within this particular lifetime and destiny. Also according to how much we are connected to our guides and intuitions.

As souls, we feel the energy pull us whenever we are guided most intensely towards our destiny. Destiny is a pact and a guide but not a rule. We are never ruled except by our choices.

Dear Flame ...

Do You Know How Much We Really Are To Each Other

...

The Memories

Many things bring up the memories that keep our connection alive. It can be a movie, television, witnessing others in situations or even just the smell of a flower. Memories flood in. I'm committed to only letting in the joyful, beautiful memories that made us who we are.

There are those things, like how when our first born was only a year old she went through a period of not wanting to sleep in her cot. You would drive her around in the car to bring on the soothing hum of the motor and she would fall asleep. We got through this period by not obsessing over it. But all the wonderful things you did for our family — those memories are ingrained into my heart.

The memories keep flooding in now. Everything we ever did together was love and magic. My thoughts of those memories touch my heart today, right now. I sometimes think of that very long period when I was asleep. I was not in reality. I can't, right now, fathom how it all happened to me. It happened to all of us. I'm so very sorry but it's still acceptance and still part of the destiny. The reunion is the healing of an entire family.

The fact is that something happened to me that blinded me. It knocked me over and no-one knew or noticed. No-one I knew saw it for what it was. How could they if I didn't see it myself? Something opened up that was meant to open and I slipped through the cracks of life. That's the only way I can describe how I lost my mate and my flame for so long. At the same time you also lost that loving feeling and connection. You did not in any way see this as possibly being a split for us. I see that clearly. It was still a shock to you but it was still an inevitable and spiritual guidance for us to learn from and continue on to a more passionate and heavenly reunion.

If only you had realised. I was unwell. I made the wrong decisions. I look back now and see that I was a different person to the one I am today. I would never make those decisions now. That comes from the learning. That is the dawning. Here is where I recognise the twin flame existence and why the break has to occur in some relationships. Instead of going down that 'if only' trail it's beneficial to look back and see the learning and the inevitability of it all. You see I would not be who I am today to look back and not recognise my actions back then — if I had not gone through the darkness and apparent loss.

I now have the chance, well actually the destiny, to go Home. Home is my heart and it's also your heart. You're my forever into eternity MATE.

Home is You.

The Cutting Off

When I first 'ran' and the split occurred you pursued me and you were angry. I only now understand all this. You eventually met someone else and formed a relationship. You both directed anger to me. This new person egged you on and contributed to your further anger. She did not help you or even love you. She was using you. She was not for you at all. I felt this deeply and wished I had not added to you being in this vulnerable position. After this second relationship broke up for you, you then met someone else. You got married again.

You never even mentioned this marriage to any of your own children. They were in the dark and this person did not even like or welcome your children.

This person encouraged you to break away from your family. She was also a jealous controller. She also could not possibly have loved you. Love never harms. There was a long split time here when it appeared that you had abandoned our children.

During this time you went into the mode of blocking me from your life. Fair enough, I now realise, because you were very hurt. I was also not in the thinking position of noticing this or feeling any harm from it. You also tried to hide your actual address even from your own dear children. They were bewildered during this time of your marriage to this person.

I cried for you during this time. You eventually woke up to all this and left her. You realised you had lost your children along the way. You then made advances to repairing this. You would eventually acknowledge that 'we' could attend family functions and other places together. This is the time during which I was starting to wake up and I realised that we were still connected and always would be. I could have gone back then but I was not fully awake yet. The connection was there and the fire inside was smouldering unseen and unnoticed.

There was then a time of many years when you were in 'our' lives. Your children and my second marriage. I'm quite sure it still ran deep the 'hatred' towards my second partner. You had spoken of it when we first split. But on the surface you showed platitude. I had started to feel anticipation whenever I knew I would see you at functions. It ran very deep. So deep I didn't recognise it even to myself but I felt it. I knew it was there. There are many "if onlys" now when I know I'm now in the 'return' faze. I know it would not have worked out for the deep fire and passion even back then and I must be content to know that I have now reached that explosive stage. The time is right. I must always be calm and know this right now.

Now that, at the current time, you are in another relationship that appears to make you very happy you have once again blocked me out of your life. I only have one avenue whereby I can actually contact you. Social media is blocked. This happened suddenly and recently. I don't know your reasoning behind it. I'm unaware if something happened to bring about this action. I can assume with intuition that maybe it was requested by someone else. But I can't be sure. But I do know you block me when you are unsure and when you think I'm not there for you. It actually brings me strong faith in that you still love me as your lifelong love. If you had indifference towards me, you would not protest by blocking me. It shows your true love runs deep and is hurt. I have to endure this with good faith. I need to have ongoing faith in the stars and faith in our destiny. The destiny is set in motion already. It can't be ignored or blocked out.

The fact that I got caught up in the new relationship that came about for me at the time of our split turned out to be a problem I could not find a way out of. It was a huge problem in my life. It was the decreed challenge of the Twin Flame relationship. We both had these challenges. Many people in these same situations will react as I did. I did nothing. Yes, I did nothing when I could have acted and changed everything. It was not to be, of course. I can easily look back now with retrospection. At the time years ago when I realised I needed you, the one I'm connected to, I thought it was too late and that you had moved on.

I was caught in something I would come to realise was a trap. Nothing worked out how I imagined it would. Well, that statement can sum up life. We are born unaware and need to wake up during our lifetime here. Well, the trap was set and I fell in.

It's been a rocky road going to places I never would have chosen to go but it's like I was hanging on for my dear life on a roller coaster and I couldn't let go or I would not learn everything I learnt. Life has been a frightening ride in adulthood but now it's calm again because I know where I will be ending up. One major thing I learnt – I know who my Twin Flame is and I know where the passion of my life is now. Without this learning curve I could have let it pass me by.

How Did It Happen?

For years I've wondered how this major break between us happened. I have now found the answers to that. My memory fades a bit as it seems so long ago. But the fact is that we stopped supporting each other all those years ago. We didn't even realise we were doing that. The stuff of life got in the way and we were both naive and unprepared for stressful events.

All sorts of life events came up for us as they do for everyone. The birth of children, the health problems, job losses, bills to pay and just rushing and rushing around. All the time a gap was appearing between us. We could not see. We were blind to the events going on. We were still always and forever connected under all of this — in a place we could no longer see. But it is this connection that meant we could never actually break apart. The unseen cord connected us still. On and on it will be and it can't be stopped.

That part where I thought I was not seeing you still. Yes, the part where it seemed like 'out-of-sight' 'out-of-mind' was happening to me. You still loved me all along. But I seemed to be in a very deep chasm. I had even made a promise to myself that I would never go through a break in a relationship like that again. Because we are Twin Flames the break was so very damaging to us. I cried for 2 years at first. So I imagined that this new second marriage would be successful and never break. I told myself I could never have that damaging break again. I was so wrong about that. It actually could never continue on. The Twin Flame was there all the time and it was always inevitable that we return to each other. Destiny calls and tells us strongly to turn to each other.

The years and years I stayed on not being happy at all. Many times they seemed wasted years to me but of course it was all about how long it took me to learn life lessons and wake up. I've been slow at life lessons this lifetime and many times I recognised that I did some life events twice before I learnt. It's been a pattern in my life. Slow but sure. Because I've been slow and doing things twice I have learnt on a far better and higher level. I now notice and acknowledge this fact.

The longer the pain we go through then the more intense is the passion and fire of our reunion and healing. I need to be grateful and accepting of this. I had imagined happiness would be there this second time. I had not bargained for the pull of a Twin Flame. I was, back then, still unaware of this. If I had realised about our twin flame relationship then I would have known any secondary relationships we may have gone through would always be wrong and not a completion for us.

Yes, there were two marriages. My repeat pattern. But I needed to recognise that there needed to also be two breaks. This last break is me returning Home and to the Flame.

As I write this book the flame inside me burns brighter, bigger and hotter. I could just run to you right now if the time was right. I am impatient. I must calm myself. If I heard from someone — anyone — that you have broken your recent relationship and you are once again alone then I would run to you so fast I would be breathless. Destiny demands that your recent relationship will fade away. It doesn't need to be dramatic or painful for anyone involved. It will simply fade and the break in those connecting cords will be so soft that it won't even hurt.

A number of instances came up that made me aware this second marriage wasn't what I had thought. I actually could have woken up then but I stayed in the mode of not wanting anymore breaks in my life. I wasn't brave enough then. I am certainly very brave now. The true and final catalyst for my commitment to return to you was my own heart disease. It was a shock but through it all I could now see how our scars matched up. We both had our hearts opened up and stopped and then they were sewn back up. They matched. But also the trauma of the knowledge of this illness caused me to hurry up the process and also to recognise it. It was in my face and I could no longer ignore any of it.

I'm now brave enough to take bold steps. These bold steps could put me in jeopardy of failure and humiliation. But I do not care about this. To me this possibility can't even exist.

Looking back I can even say by the time of the third anniversary in my second partnership I knew things weren't right. This was not a successful relationship at all. I had practiced many new things to keep it alive. Wedding photos on the wall, wedding album, preserved wedding flowers framed and on the wall. Down the track after awakening I was to take these all down and store them away. I could not look at them on the wall when they were not reminders of my true love. I wasn't, back then, confident enough to break free. I inappropriately felt obligated to stay. This situation certainly did not send the right messages to my true love, my flame.

You know, you have had at least three new relationships since we split. You have married once more and thought about marrying again a third time. This is all because you miss 'us' and your desires are to go towards being connected to love. You are just mistaken in not realising that your desires are for us to return home together. Once you are fully awake to that there will be no stopping us. We will burn together once more and no-one can ever come between us again. I burn for you.

If only I had known about your second marriage ending so soon after. Six months, but I thought it had been around ten years. My own second marriage was ending around the same time. The writing was on the wall for it to end but I kept on blindly going with it. If I had somehow been in touch to know your situation things would have changed back then. But in my heart of hearts I also know that the learning would not have been complete then. There was more to it — longer to go — much to occur.

I recall in those middle years of separation how at functions we both attended — yes, how you introduced me with pride to people you knew as 'your ex-wife'. I saw your pride and wished for things to be different then.

~~~

You Have Returned To Me
My True Love
Because You Never
Really Left Me

...

Spiritual and Emotional
Cords Still Bind Us
In Pure Love

...

CHAPTER 7

THE AWAKENING

I'm sure you were awake for years to our real connection. Perhaps not awakened on a spiritual level yet. I was asleep then. I needed you to be stronger and push towards me then but you eventually backed off and married again. As I also did myself ... you chose a difficult partner.

I completely understand why you gave up. I took too long. You were hurt. We eventually swapped places of the runner and the chaser. I became a silent inactive chaser for many years.

It's now been a lot of years and I have fully awakened to our connection. But now you seem to be insulated against this knowledge. You have closed yourself up from it. It's been a long lesson for us changing along the way from who is the chaser and who is the runner. The fact that I'm now fully awake to everything right now means I can participate in practices that can open your eyes this time also.

Look for the Signs Along the Way

I already know my current marriage is not working. It's really just a friendship or companionship now.

Just living together to save money, for convenience and all that. Something I can't get out of until that moment in time when destiny is unlocked. It will be a time that is noticed like an electric shock. All the work towards reunion will suddenly click and all kinds of things will be released all at once. Bells will ring and stars will shine brightly.

The signs must be looked for if you want to fulfil your destiny. They must be acted on when your awakened state has seen them. Once you have realised you are part of a Twin Flame relationship you can't go back. You can't stop the progress towards reunion. But at the same time you must act in alignment with it all.

I have actually made the movements towards you to show that I am open to changes. You know some of the very basic facts but have not acted. You won't necessarily know how to act on this new information I have given to you. Although I am currently sometimes blocked you have agreed on two occasions to meet with me privately. The first time it was on the occasion of our previous date of the anniversary of our original wedding.

You gave me some information on that occasion (even though you were by now in this more recent relationship) that broke my heart and brought tears to my eyes. You told me that you had loved me deeply and that you would never marry again. But only a relatively short time later you and your new partner had an engagement party. I felt you had told me false information. But ... there will not be a wedding at all. This shows me you can awaken. The other occasion was because I had been given some not good news about my health. I asked to meet to discuss the future of our children and how I would like to leave any of my assets to them.

I also wrote and printed a letter for you that outlined how my state of affairs currently was and how I realised a number of things about us. I did not choose to give this letter to you because I did not want anything written on paper that could be ever accessed by another person.

You read it and I still have it because I said to you it will stay in my possession. I presume you now understand many things about me and about us. But not everything even if you took it in when reading the letter. I did what I needed to do because it was uncertain if I would live through a major surgery coming up or even much longer after that.

I have now learnt to speak my mind when it is vitally important. This heart disease and serious open heart surgery taught me to be brave and speak my mind before it's too late. Destiny is so important it can go ahead and change your life situation without you even being aware it's happening. Learn to be brave when it matters most.

It was during that year when I found out about my health conditions — the shock of the state of my physical heart — that I started to fully wake up to the Twin Flame situation we are both in. I saw it all with clarity. We have now both had open heart surgery to save our lives. We have the matching scars on our hearts.

These two scars need to be welded together and matched in life right now. It all proves that although our hearts can be broken, they can be mended. So also can our children's hearts be mended with our reunion.

I also met up with an old friend recently who has been a friend to both of us for many years. Among many other things discussed at our meetup was an astounding unexpected statement she made to me.

Astounding because it confirms that our reunion will take place. Also astounding because it confirms I'm on the right track and it's something I never had heard from you myself. She said that she attended your recent engagement and that you told her that I am your one true love and that it will never be like that for you with anyone else. This is fairly recent and it was at your engagement. This is very telling. It encourages me to go ahead with all the plans I have made to make my way towards you and not away from you as in the past.

It also means there is a new marriage on the cards that will definitely take place. It will be a celebration of life and reunion and atonement. But it is not a marriage with your current new partner. No chance of that in our destiny. But be assured that there is definitely a marriage coming up soon and it is ours.

The plans and destiny are already taking place right now. Various situations and actions have already taken place and are waiting for this day. Not only will it be new for us, it will also be a recreation.

The various preparations on a spiritual level have already changed fate, time and space for many people.

Bring Us To That Place

To
That Place
Where We Belong
Together

...

New Daily Existence

My life going forward is very different now. I see daily the new life and the reunion. Each day I incorporate where I see myself living rather than where I seem to currently be. I look away from my current life to 'be' in the new one.

Self talk: This is not my life — not my existence. I can even see the house and room I am going into. I put myself there daily. I see myself daily in your house with you but I also see that we will combine our assets and purchase a home that is ours alone with no memories of past partners in it. It's a brand new beginning for both of us.

Although I saw myself as being necessary in that second person's life — in the way of helping to advance and show how to heal for that person — I also now see I have finished. I have done all that I can do for now. As that person now rejects any further healing or help, I can leave in peace now. It was not a match in romance or fire in the first place. I just was mistaken in thinking that's what it was originally. That mistake was for the sake of healing for all concerned. It was a major soul mate meeting for the purpose of soul advancement of all concerned.

I can't allow myself to feel I'm leaving any unfinished business behind. I must go into my reunion with flow and love. I cannot allow any kind of sorry feelings when I move out of my current life and into the familiar but new life. Those familiar feelings of connection, that are now complete, mean no more feelings of fear or lack. Those feelings that made me run away in the first place.

This time I'm not running away but simply leaving behind something that no longer serves me or anyone else. This time I'm running towards. Towards my true love and my true twin flame life. I am running towards contentment and creativity and towards life itself.

There can now be no other way. As if I'm ever going to die with that flame still burning in me. I cannot pass from this life and you can't either till our flames reconnect and make a bigger fire.

The more I write — the more I create. You can do this too for yourself and your own journey. Write it all down. Create it as you go.

If there's one thing I've learnt from this whole lifetime and circumstances — it is that I can do anything. You can do anything. We can do anything. It's all up to us what we create and who we are. What our lives will be. Choose.

We learn a lot from these lifetimes. After leaving that first time with a split from you, my twin flame, I firstly became quite ill and was hospitalised. It affected my lungs that time. An indication I had chosen to find it hard to breathe without you.

Later as I settled into a new life with a new partner I eventually became ill with two serious chronic diseases. The first one that appeared was diabetes. The meaning here was: The sweetness had left my life. Years later heart disease appeared. It does take years to get to that point of disease. The meaning here was: My heart was broken many years ago.

I believe that when we are reunited that I have the chance to heal even from those serious physical diseases. So do you. These are diseases that doctors will tell you are not only chronic but that they advance with the years. Well, I'm choosing not to believe that.

I'm Falling Into Confusion

I'm falling ... I'm falling. I'm wide awake right now. That explains the confusion. How was I blind to so much for so long? I had fallen so far down that there was no option but to look upwards and aim for love and reunion. There was also no option but to believe anything is possible.

This explains the story. That also explains our life and our destiny. I just need to catch up on it all and recognise that so much has been guided all through our lives here.

The Car Show Tears

I could have run away with you anytime during those years. I was in that frozen state where I could not make a move. I still had not convinced myself it was wise to have another break and go to you. I also was unsure of your feelings. I'm now sure.

Now I can move and I can speak no matter if I'm feeling foolish or I risk actually being foolish. I no longer care. Why? Because I only care about the truth, taking risks and our love.

The Waiting Time

I sometimes wonder how we can survive this time of waiting to be together. Wherever you go I will be waiting for you. Whatever it takes we can be assured that the destiny will be the completion of us.

I wait and I am accepting of the waiting time. I wait for you to fully awaken. It is our pact and can never not be.

The ego fear is the one thing that can be in the way of any reunion. Both of us have to put this ego away. We need to focus on each other on the soul level. Our souls are one. The ego tries to make us fear change and fear forgiveness.

Oh, let my love be strong enough — to take away the pain and heartache and soothe the longing for you.

Now and forever we are together. I seem to lose my way when I don't see you here near me. But I will always find it again when I know you are waiting for me forever. Now and forever you will be my man — my other half — the other half of our one soul.

Until the time this Earth stops spinning and far beyond even that — we are together — we have completed the destiny circle. We are joined once more. Until even the ocean stops touching the sand — which far into the future of existence it may stop — but far even beyond that we are still 'one soul'.

We Return Every Lifetime

We will be in every possibility, in all directions of time and space and in every timeline and lifetime.

We will always be, for eternity, to join in love as One. You are The One.

~~~

If it's not forever

Then it's not love

...

The White Knight Story

And The White Knight felt the energy shift and awakened to his life purpose and true path. He was incredulous at first. How was he asleep all those years? Way back before birth in this lifetime they made the pact.

They would meet and instantly recognise each other but only on the subconscious level. All the same they still knew on the conscious level — that they were meant to be.

A little bit into this story he strayed for a short time. She looked away and did not pursue. She walked away but he suddenly woke up again and ran after her. They reunited. Their story then flowed on. Magic. The white lace and tulle.

All so beautiful together. But still of the naive world, they blindly went through the ups and downs of human life. Like all Twin Flames they eventually had a large break that went for a long time.

Ogres appeared in their lives posing as angels

Then towards the end of this lifetime they awoke one at a time and realised the circle about to be joined. They were touched by the pink energy and the red flame. Their hearts now matched with the repairs showing at the front of their matching bodies. Those hearts fused together with the hot flame of heaven.

...

I Love You More Than Words
Could Ever Say

I Love You Yesterday
I Love You Today

...

CHAPTER 8

OUR REUNION

Life turned sour it seemed, but now it's time to make it sweet!

When – NOW! Always think in the now when manifesting anything in your 'Desires'.

The only thing left on this planet in this physical world and beyond is: "You and Me". We match and blend.

We are One! In the time of Now!

The Reunion is clearly a very important time in the lives of the Twin Flames and the culmination of a lifetime's work towards it. Some will never make it to the reunion at all. They may miss the connections and the subtle spiritual messages coming their way throughout their lives. No matter — it will still occur as they are both connected forever.

Nothing compares in either of our entire lifetimes to this 'Reunion' that is only our experience. It is the One experience for both of us that stands out as the moment we were born for.

Our Own Reunion

Now that I know it's inevitable, I have to curb my impatience. I have to await the time that you are Awakened to everything that we are to each other.

I feel the energies wanting to burst forth from within me. That wanting to get a move on and flee to you my love and reunite right now. There must be acceptance and patience for it all to work. This I must remember daily. I keep getting the feeling of a need to sort through my current life, get rid of clutter and objects and even start to pack some essential items so that I'm ready when the time becomes clear to me.

I kept three important and symbolic items from our Twin Flame passion of years ago. They were from our first joining. These items would turn out to be catalysts for the awakening and the reuniting. It wasn't even deliberate that I kept them. Obviously on a subconscious level they were meant to remain in my clear possession for later use.

What are they? Do I reveal that? Yes. Two gold rings (one a diamond ring) and a wedding album.

You see, the fact that I kept these symbolic items even without being consciously aware as to why I did, means something incredibly important. The fact that they survived at least four house moves in all that time apart is also a miracle in itself. I've never been good on the surface at remembering where I put or store things. So they've survived of their own accord (apparently) and still they are here right now.

Everyone will have their own story to tell. Even if you only tell it to yourself. We sometimes seek outside of ourselves for our story that is inside us.

We Belong To Us

No-one can interfere with us. I am in you and you are within me. We are as One. We belong to Us only. There is an awful thought: **'what if I'd never known you'**. My whole life would have been worth nothing to me. I can't imagine or bear the thought of having lived this life without you.

Life could never have been beautiful without you

'The White Knight Story', following Chapter 7, is a burning piece of fire and insight that describes our twin flame story. I simply love to read and re-read this little 'fairy story' I wrote and created. You are my 'White Knight'.

I've always had a love of fairy stories and whatever you choose to believe in life is true for you. Believe in yourself and believe in your Twin Flame. That's all that is needed for it to culminate in 'The Fire' of passion.

Believe in the Story. We all have one.

It's Not About I'm Leaving

It's about I'm going to something. I'm going to someone. It's about I'm going to you. I'm returning to Love. My life is changing before my very eyes. It's changing into my own creation and back to the pact we both made. It is not focussing on leaving something or someone. It's not about leaving — it's about going and rejoining. This knowing can sustain you until your destiny is fulfilled.

121

It's hard to get agreement in this world between friends or lovers. We all talk a different language. The healing is about how we will all understand each other one day. That day is coming for us.

Many of us do not even give each other time. All we have here on Earth is time. Time to spend on each other. But the world is too busy. It all passes over everyone and they do not notice others enough. We can all slow down and stop to smell the roses each day.

We can all listen as well as hear. Hearing is one thing and listening, really listening is completely another thing.

The Fire Will Burn

There are many connections, passions and love actions to be played out. We both have so much fire in us but in our former years together I can't get a feel for whether we loved with abandonment or not. I don't think we were free in our minds to let go like that.

We are now ready and it must be completed. It's in the destiny of our incarnation. We still have time to let go with this abandonment. It will free us and spiral us up through the vortex of time and positive light energy.

Our love will catch fire and burn for eternity. We will have that chance now to let go and allow the passions of our freedom to burn on and manifest into the passions of human interactions.

Our reunion is the completion of our pact together and puts us on a new path to walk together.

The Catalyst For Reunion

There is self healing and a turning time when you will enable the reunion by your love for everything. I reached a point in this second relationship whereby I stopped fighting against how things were. I had recognised our destiny was already set for us. It simply needed this recognition to set it all in motion.

I started to realise I was deeply unhappy and that I could change that. I decided one day that it's about showing love to everyone around you and not dwelling in the unhappiness of any current relationship.

This decision has changed everything and also the way the destiny will play out. There was a last day of anguish and fighting against my situation. I lashed out in anger and spoke of leaving everything behind and going my own way. By the end of that day I realised how to change it all. No matter what your situation — show love for everyone. Except when it is clear you do need to leave.

Passing By Places We Went

Memories tug at me and pull me into a vortex of wonder. I can access you anytime when they do. I feel you close now and over the past many years I did still always feel you. You never left my thoughts.

When I see all these places and things that remind me, it's always of you and no-one else but you.

You're as beautiful to me today as you were all those years ago.

This is the connection of twin flames that never goes away.

There's no way we can continue to deny each other. Any other people surrounding us must give way to the destiny. That's because our destiny and theirs is also connected. It is connected to ours because those others must give way to our pact and they must fade into our backgrounds. They each need to follow their own destiny.

We will follow through no matter what comes our way. As long as we focus on the outcome, the healing and the love.

Both houses our parents originally lived in are still standing today. These are the two houses we walked between so many times holding hands.

The Choosing

I will be asking you to 'choose' very soon. After you have heard and read the many words I have written about us here in this book, there will come the choosing time.

I will be direct and I will give you all that I have in relation to 'us'. This will be a telling time for you and it will affect the twin flame relationship for the rest of this lifetime.

I will be asking — do you know who the real love of your life is? I will be asking — please think carefully and weigh up all the options for us all. If you do know, and you have become aware, then it's time for changes to be made.

Who is also giving you everything you need? Is anything being held back in any current relationship? Do you live together and share all assets and all of yourself?

If you choose to be brave and change your life and be in reunion with your twin flame then you are also fulfilling those wishes you had when we first split and during the running period when you were the chaser. You will win back your true love after all. We are both winners.

Just remember that day is coming when you will come to pick me up and I have my suitcases with me — that is the day you have dreamed of. That day has come to us now — the day I ran away was the day I was confused and my memory and senses left me for a few years.

I did not recognise the truth of who we are to each other. It can no longer be denied now.

It seems like we could both choose the safe life — the one where we let fear of change in. We could stay in our current lives and just be comfortable but unhappy. We now have to choose change over fear.

If you choose to change your life and be in reunion with your twin flame then you are also fulfilling those wishes you had when we first split and during the running period when you were the chaser. You will now receive your greatest desires.

It shall be — "Do You Choose Fire and Passion and Destiny?" Your answers will affect both of us.
Think deeply.

Growth

The most accelerate growth in my lifetime was when we had separated. This seems so bitter-sweet now. But it is so.

I have learnt so much and forgiven so much of myself and of you also that we can now enjoy the most passionate, fiery but peaceful love we could ever have known. Once we have both learnt all we need to know and accepted each other once again and forever more — that's when we reap all the benefits of this lifetime.

All major change in life seems impossible until it becomes inevitable. This is the same in all world evolutionary circumstances. It is also the same with twin flame relationships and reunions.

There Were So Many Places
Back then ... there were so many places you went to that I was also attending over the years. You turned up for me so many times but I was still blinded then. I admit I was stirred by your presence.

I can't possibly, in the present time, relate to who I was back then in our 40s. I can't relate to decisions I made back then. That wasn't the real me. I hope you can understand this fact. More than anything I would like you to know this. In the completion of the atonement these facts I can't relate to will be dissolved.

Loneliness
We will both be forever lonely if we don't complete our reunion. No matter whether we have any other secondary relationship in our lives that we believe is a true love. It can never be our true love and flame connection. No other person can ever be connected to us in the way we are. It's about recognising this fact.

We both have to realise this loneliness will follow us and creep up on us whenever there is a crack in our armour of life. It can only be cured and resolved through the reunion and the reigniting of our soul.

This mountain we must climb, we must climb it together. The thought of it can seem like the whole world is on our shoulders. But in actual fact this mountain can disappear as soon as we look directly at it and see the true facts. As soon as we stop looking away and seeing the wrong life story. Once we are both awake and see the truth.

Why Couldn't I Have Seen You

Why couldn't I, back then, have seen you and your reality? Years and years ago and when we first met and were so very young. That's the you I lost sight of but I see it all now so clearly.

I see you. I feel you. I smell that special scent of your inner self. When I see, feel and breathe you, then I am you. We are One.

Love Needs A Meeting

Love needs a meeting where we can talk freely and truthfully and from the heart. A meeting where we hide nothing even from ourselves. We only get very few opportunities to do this in life. It takes great courage to go ahead and meet and speak the truth.

Please read 'our' book and then tell me how you really feel after that. Yes, I mean really. We don't, any of us, have that many years left to put everything right. Rejoin the circle. Reunite the Twin Flames as it is pacted by our destinies.

What is pacted and desired strongly using the Law of Attraction to its utmost will always Be. Whatever you create in your mind and believe in your heart cannot ever not Be. That is the Law of Creation.

Looking Through The Eyes of Love

Yes. I now see you through the eyes of love. Once again and forevermore. I'm looking through pure love. I'm not looking at illusions or being deceived by other intervening people.

All those years of thinking my life was one way when it was always the opposite to what I thought I saw.

All Our History Still Exists

And it's not bad at all. It's all good. There are the most amazing of memories from our early years. Those years when things started to decline I now see they all concerned our lack of awakening and naivety. The ill health could have been dealt with if we had accessed our pure love. We simply did not have that knowledge then. We gained that knowledge from the painful split.

The greater amount of moments are beautiful and lasting. They are filled with the fire of passion. You were the One. You are the One.

That Moment In Time

That moment in time when I could have avoided the painful break. I see it clearly now. But it's not to be looked at because it was necessary.

Because that would then preclude both of us from the learning and the healing. Our choices were made long ago when the pact was made.

I still sometimes think to myself: "You should have continued to pursue me back then". But perhaps if you had continuously pursued me I would never have woken up at all. It is always the pain and learning that wakes us all up. Wishful thinking and wishing things were different will only harm your focus and course of action.

I do see you continued pursuing me but in a quieter non proactive way. I see it now. I know why you lost confidence in the whole pursuit. But because that's not really part of our story and it's actually a much longer story than that, then I must still retain faith in the real path.

I realise I followed you nearly all of this time. Over the years I always wanted to be where you were and to see you, notice you and be with you. I subconsciously tried to deny this to myself.

We were, all this time, trying to get back to each other. If you look very closely you will realise the relationship you went into towards the end of our break time is not the love of your life. Always ask that question of yourself.

Any other relationship you may be in is because you were lonely and someone coming into your life was your opportunity. It's not the love of your life at all.

Choose to make a decision that is not based in fear. It's hard to choose to change your life completely in the latter years. But do you choose some kind of happiness and easing of loneliness OR do you choose to be brave and go back to your true love and be joyful every part of every day?

The same first love we had all those years ago can be ours again today. But it will be enhanced by the separation, the learning and the passionate fire of the reunion. It can get no better than this in anyone's lifetime. It's about awakening and choosing. It's about your true love reigniting.

Yesterday, today, forever

When we are awake we see them all as one. We only need to now choose our lives as we wish them to be. When we see a beautiful sunset we can walk together into it now. Run away with me!

Passing By Places We Went

Memories tug at me and pull me into a vortex of wonder. I can access you anytime when they do. I feel you close now and over the past many years I did still always feel you. You never left my thoughts.

When I see all these places and things that remind me it's always of you and no-one else but you.

You're as beautiful to me today as you were all those years ago. This is the connection of twin flames that never goes away.

We will always see the beauty in each other and in our connection and our destiny.

There's no way we can continue to deny each other. Any other people surrounding us must give way to the destiny. That's because our destiny and theirs is also connected. It is connected to ours because those others must give way to our pact and they must fade into our backgrounds.

We will follow through no matter what comes our way. As long as we focus on the outcome, the healing and the love.

This Is Not A Transient Romance

That is not us. We are 'The Flame'. It is a huge privilege to be in a sacred flame relationship. We are also influencing world evolvement. Our relationship did not slowly develop from a long term friendship (like many people). That's not even a true romance when that happens. It is usually merely a convenience for both parties. Their own perception of their aloneness propels them into a romance with a long term friend. That kind of relationship is never 'On Fire' with passions that take them far away and seem almost 'out of body'. It's also clear that this kind of relationship can never be called a twin flame. There wasn't a flame in the first place.

It's Not All Roses

The twin flame relationship is not always rose coloured. This is especially just before the separation. It has by then deteriorated badly. This is all illusion of course. As, of course, we are both divine beings.

What makes a person or couple divine? Divine means the existence of a spiritual presence or pact within a place, person, thought or life path. Twin flames are divine by the very idea that they are spiritually blessed and destined in spirit before appearing here on Earth in humanity.

The true flame and the glow of this relationship comes after the Reunion. That is what the reunion is for. You will access unconditional love, joy, healing and abundance in your life.

After all the rain and after all the pain — it becomes the fire, the love and the glow of balance.

The Places We Will Go To

Once our reunion has taken place there will be places to go and reignite memories.

We will go to Oakleigh, Huntingdale, Springvale and Sorrento. We will revisit all those beautiful times together.

It is written in my heart and I can speak a prophecy for you that we will marry again. Last and forever in this lifetime. In the same church. The Church of Emmanuel. We will be fulfilling our destiny on that day.

Once in every lifetime comes a love like ours.

I Love You more than the world
Always Have
Always Will!

~~~

It is written

Indelibly on the universal field

...

We are reuniting, rejoining and reigniting

...

Any partners we turned to in the past or at the present time

They will fade

Our Light will dim them

...

CHAPTER 9

TRUE STORIES

I have come across many relationships of other people in my lifetime. They have inspired me in so many ways. Many could be called Twin Flame relationships or Soul Mates. On examination of the details, they can all quite possibly be called Twin Flames. Let us scrutinise some of them:

Tilly and Keith

This couple met in the marvellous 60s. Living in London was exciting back then. Being born then was a life full of fashion, hair and the huge success of the music and bands. This couple were into the clothes, the music scene and riding around on a Vespa motorcycle. This was all so 'in' then. Say what you will here. But these two were devoted from day one when they first laid eyes on each other.

They met, as many do, by almost running into each other one day. It was a whirlwind romance and their devotion knew no bounds. They married young (as many did back then) and had two children. They had a girl, then a boy. Life seemed magical then for this family and the couple.

Later in life, yes they did have a split. This was not in the traditional way of a marriage or relationship separation. That was never to be for this couple. It just couldn't happen. But there was a split all the same. It came in the form of a major rare illness. One of the partners came to get a condition that caused early onset dementia. What a huge blow for this couple. It meant that one would go into another world of their own and that the other would be left alone with barely a connection left.

But did this mean an end to their relationship? Absolutely not. Keith never wavered from his devotion. He refused to allow her to go into any kind of nursing care. She deteriorated over a 7 year period. Even though she was given a life span of only about 3 years after diagnosis. His decisions and actions lengthened her life by more than double.

At first he worked his own business around her being in the house for short periods and it worked out ok. Eventually he left his business and sold their house to travel around the country with her. He purchased a mobile home and fitted it out to suit her needs. Travelling the country and showing her things of nature and beauty even though it appeared she could not fathom anything around her. This life went on for a number of years. His devotion lengthened her lifetime by many years.

Eventually she was to die and leave him temporarily. This is how this particular couple's split and chase was different. It appears she left involuntarily with this illness but in fact it was planned on a spiritual level. He made a life for himself after that of a kind. Not one he loved in any way. It was alone mostly. He always kept a dog or two around him for comfort. He settled in a coastal town and lived his life. He is currently back with her in the afterlife as he succumbed to the covid virus in 2020. He had made the request 'not to be resuscitated' with hospital staff. After a few weeks in hospital with the virus that swept the entire world, he slipped away, into her arms.

Jane and Robert

This couple met in the 50s. The days of rock and roll's birth. They were a beautiful couple, her long black hair and full skirts of the 50s making for a great scene. Life was just starting for them at the time.

After a whirlwind of courtship and going to places together they married quite young. This was in their late teens. They set up their life in an iconic beachside suburb and soon had their first child, a girl. Within a short time they had a boy also. This is when they had some trouble getting by in life and he found it hard to get work. Her parents helped to find them a house in a country town and he found work. They had two more children but a far better setting for them all to grow up in.

Unfortunately (and of course spiritually planned unknown to them) his parents had set him up for a difficult life. They were both alcoholics and over a number of years he succumbed to the same problems.

This eventually brought about that twin flame 'split'. She asked him to leave and he did. Leaving that family as a single parent unit. Times were hard and got even harder. The family stayed in a country town environment during all their growing up time. They had moved around to a few different towns and eventually settled into one particular area.

They both went through deep dark times during this split. He went down a trail that led him to ill-health. He had lost his entire family and felt the pain. He eventually went out and searched for her.

She met another partner and settled down with him. It was not to work out here either and there was a huge traumatic breakup in this second relationship also. Far worse than her initial break-up with her twin flame. Life had turned nasty but she got on with it. Although this relationship lasted quite a few years and there were children from it — this new relationship was no twin flame but a learning experience.

Many, many years later when she was living on her own with one of her adult sons in this town she settled into — some kind of miracle occurred. Her Twin Flame turned up and told her he had been looking for her for many, many years. It must have been at least 30 years of being apart. He had been searching for her for a long time. He had healed many of his former problems with health and drinking. I personally don't know his full story while he was apart from her or how he found her but she did still use by her original married name with him. There was much celebrating and a magical photo of them together at this rejoining that is still in existence.

Unfortunately, he was only back with her for a few weeks when he had a stroke — possibly connected to his long term drinking. He ended up in a nursing care facility and by this time she was getting older and had quite a few health problems herself. She was unable to look after him by now. A relative of his took him away to another town hundreds of miles away and got him into a nursing home there. He was virtually unable to care for himself by then.

He died in that town and was buried there. She struggled on in life with her illnesses that had by now become quite serious. There was breast cancer and diabetes. Although she came through surgery and chemotherapy with strength she didn't know she had — at the five year point after chemotherapy she had cancer spread into other vital areas like liver and bones. She eventually passed away and joined him once again. I know they are now together and healed.

Gerry and Eva

This couple is a classic example of Twin Flames that only meet late in life and do not necessarily have any kind of 'split'. They have both already been through a number of relationships that they have learned many lessons from. They may both have already healed their past traumas through other relationships. Then they become ready to meet in this lifetime. With this couple it is obvious they are Twin Flames and their lives are parallel and on the same level. No-one could possibly ever come between them.

I find this phenomenon amazingly good and natural. They have both spent long years without even meeting. Gerry was well into his late 60s when they met and Eva in her late 40s. They love to do everything together every day. This does not mean they have never had a disagreement as they are both individuals with differences — otherwise they could not have an interesting lifetime together. They have different talents that they can express themselves through and that makes them both complete in their relationship. They truly balance each other. They also both have matching talents that they utilise together. Both have walked away from previous relationships and the past to live in the moment of today. That is a sure sign that joy flourishes.

Both have had traumas in the past and have gone beyond them. If you manage to go beyond your past traumas and they no longer inflict any kind of pain on you then you have healed them. That is why some twin flame relationships do not need to go through all the stages including the painful separation.

The recognition that these two are twin flames comes not only from how they relate to each other but it is because in this relationship she is strong and a match for him. She has her say in their decisions and he is now happy for this to occur. Whereas looking back through the years, all of his relationships involved him being in charge and his partners following him but not having a true say in their lives and decisions together. Hence, all these breakups previously.

This couple is a joy to see together and they complement each other. Each takes care of the other and no argument is ever about selfishness or ego based. They are complete together and need no-one else to live joyful lives. They have a small base of close friends but these friends cannot penetrate their shell of love that surrounds them.

Bella and Grant

This couple met in middle life almost. She had been through a relationship that seemed like they were meant for each other for quite a few years. There was always a background going on whereby she had to chase a lot and he backed off a lot. They were together many years and had three children. He eventually gave in a lot to depressive moods. It was hard for her to handle and she worked regular hours for the family while he had trouble doing this.

He had nonetheless always spent time and creativity with his children. Strangely enough though after their breakup he virtually never turned up for his children again. He had a huge amount of healing to do on his own life. He delved into all sorts of things, learning, travelling and mysticism.

We can't know other people's traumas or past. No-one can really judge anything in this first relationship. Some things do seem very sad though.

No-one ever expected them to break up but yes it did happen. There was no great animosity and he just seemed to evaporate after her new true flame had arrived into her life. They all got along together for a while. Her life flame had been through a few relationships also but none of significance. He had no marriages or children to bring to this relationship.

These two are another couple who have clearly healed traumas in their previous relationships. They appear to always get along and look to each other when making important decisions. They have never had a break or gone through the various stages. These stages in twin flame relationships are only for those who have either chosen them or require them for learning.

Tammi and William

This couple met as young teenagers also. There was instant connection here. They went through their problems in life but stuck together. They made a life that they both enjoyed. They thought in similar ways. They were so young when they met that they had to keep it all a secret from their families. The parents on each side were not happy with it at first. Because of her young age mainly. No-one could, back then, see into the future or that these two were already joined before their lifetimes started here.

There eventually was one time when there was a split and a runner. It did not continue for a very long time in their case. She ran at one point when they had a young preschooler and another on the way. He had some problems with drinking that she could no longer face up to.

It became clear that he was lost during this break time. He contacted a number of friends and relatives to help him find her. One 'friend' in particular was a traitor. She gave out false information about their life together. This was ignored by those who matter. He healed his problem during the time of their split.

He was then ready to reunite and spend the rest of their lives together.

Within a fairly short time they had reunited. Before the second child was born. They have been inseparable ever since.

He has stood beside her through many years of her chronic ill-health. He has been the support and she has healed many traumas but to this day is still quite ill. Even though this is the case she is a sunny and bright personality and doesn't let any kind of illness stop her living her life. They have the same interests in life and share a hobby that is also a business.

~~~

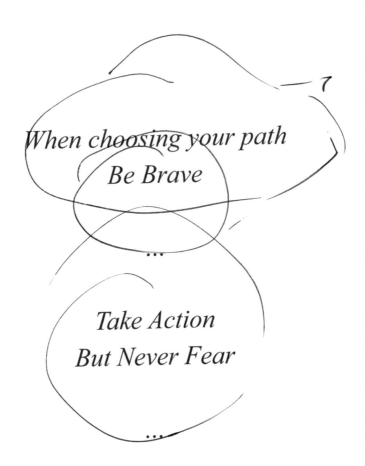

When choosing your path
Be Brave
...

Take Action
But Never Fear
...

PART THREE:

The Teachings

CHAPTER 10

PROBLEMS/SOUL FIRES

There will be many problems along the way in this lifetime together. Healing the past manifests as problems in the ego/physical world so they are unavoidable. Just always remember that nothing remains the same or stagnant forever. If you are going through a traumatic time and feel stuck in any way then it will pass and you will move into better times. Most Twin Flames will face many challenges in their lifetime.

There will be chaos, loss, pain, emotional swings, depression, obsessive thoughts, disagreements, bad timings and purging. These are absolutely all illusions. You have awakened when you see they are illusions and you pass through it all. You cannot ever lose each other and those annoying bad timings are really just for further learning.

It can look like you have missed out on reunions many times over. For instance: one will be ready to reunite and the other will seem lost and unattainable. This can occur more than once or twice.

But the bad timings will dissolve away to make way for your joining back together again.

Passion and fire in life comes from the Soul Fire within each of us. This is the fire of the soul. If you have established the facts and believe you are part of a Twin Flame relationship you can be assured that the reunion will take place and cannot be missed. No other soul can interfere with how it all plays out. It may look like others are interfering but also this is illusion.

There will be pain. There will be regrets. You cannot let those things damage you or deter you from moving on through the chaotic time and getting you through to that Reunion/Regeneration.

We must not allow the past to damage our now or our future now. The past and the memories exist for us to learn from and also for us to remember the connection and the love. Learn to filter out the past negative events. Learn to look through a pink filter of love. Tinge all that learning, the split up, the running away and the awakening with light and the colours of positive energies.

There is absolutely no doubt that many have gone through very dark times and pain. If you have recognised that you have a Twin Flame then reuniting is not an option or anything to be afraid of. It is pure Destiny and filled with Love.

Do not waste your energy trying hard to forget the bad things. Just concentrate your energies and focus on all the good memories that make up you and your flame. This means you can stay in the higher vibrations and that contributes to all your wishes coming true in your life.

Find a way to make everything ok for you right now in the present time. Even though you are working towards an event like your reunion you must still stay feeling good in the now so that you attract the good things to you constantly not just in the future that hasn't arrived yet.

The Atonement

Part of the Reunion and the Chaos will be essentially the Atonement. This means forgiveness for each other and for ourselves.

This is a major component of the entire incarnation as Twin Flames. Perhaps even the reason for it all.

It is included here in the chapter on problems and soul fires because it can be part of that struggle to find the way out.

You are me and I am you

Therefore forgiveness cannot be withheld indefinitely. Atonement and forgiveness means to recognise that no-one ever harmed anyone at all. It flows away and fades from our existence. All illusions of being harmed or having harmed another is just that — illusion. Everything was always about learning and evolvement. This major breakup was all about returning and joining the circle. When both have recognised this, then love and peace reigns in your life. This Destiny is now complete for this lifetime.

This atonement is the destiny of us all. With the twin flames existence we can look back and see parts of our life previously together and during our parting that we wish to atone for. Once we have changed the words we spoke and the actions we took — all those things we now wish to change or take back — our world and our destiny is then changed forever. It moves on into love, peace and light. Those around us will have also learnt from our own rejoining and atonement. That is part of the beauty that will surround us.

Doubts

Doubts can fill your mind during the period of your awakening when perhaps your twin flame has not yet fully woken up. You must not allow them to intrude to the point where they railroad your destiny.

If your flame has moved on temporarily and is still in a relationship that they have told themselves is 'the one' and that they are now happy — then major doubts can threaten your reunion. These doubts can take over and make you unsure of the true flame relationship. You focus only on the truth here. Know and believe that the current situation they are in will fade away. You don't have to do a single thing towards this except in your thoughts, knowledge, confidence and affirmations.

Do not, under any circumstances, try to make anything happen to complete the circle. It must, at all times, be naturally occurring. Yes, you do work on your energies and your connection. But, no you don't try to force anything in any way.

Separately we may both be weak but together we are strong. We decide our own lives — no-one can be let in to change this outcome for us. Those who have broken us apart will fade away and not be in our consciousness as we move into the reunion faze.

Do not fall into major doubt about whether your reunion will occur or not. Be assured that you would not have been led to this path in life if it was not already a foregone conclusion — a destiny and a pact.

Those Dark Times

In all the chaos and even after you have recognised the reunion is coming — there will be deep dark nights of the soul. You may sink very far down. You may wish you had never done some past actions. You may feel dark and lost over how to facilitate reunion and forgive yourself. This is the way of The Cross. The way is through pain and hurt to get to the other side.

You need to get to a place where you have let that go and where you trust implicitly in the process of destiny's fulfilment.

With the realisation of your twin flame relationship can come depression. It can come and hit you and knock you down. It's the realisation of how your life should be, compared to what it is right now. Some people feel trapped in a nothing relationship and others may be alone.

You must push through this depression because no-one ever manifested their desires from a dark place. But this dark place where you are hitting rock-bottom is the catalyst for change. It can push you up and out of the darkness. You can then be catapulted into the light unexpectedly. It then becomes all about the law of attraction — as in all aspects of life and manifesting. You must practice keeping your vibration high. Connect daily with your flame during the meditation and bring both of your vibrations to a matching level. This ensures success.

Humans Are Strange Creatures

I've very often wondered at human behaviours. How can they look at someone they think is special to them — with loving eyes that all encompass that love focus — only for that to seem to be gone years later? Where did it go? They can appear to be consumed by love for someone in their life. I've seen it. It's so special.

But ... yes, but is the word here. How can that be and then it seems to disappear? In many cases it not only disappears but it can be replaced by what humans call hate. There can be hateful conflict appearing in those previously loving relationships. There is no hate — there is only fear.

There would be some fiery relationships you would have witnessed, even if you didn't live through one. Those all consuming passionate relationships that later down the track seem to become just a dull companionship. They may even have a calm agreement about divorce. They then may go into new relationships and are comfortable with each others' choices. These relationships can seem a puzzle to some other people especially so-called romantics. But the truth is that in the first place they may have only been passionately in love with what they thought was love. Then later, the everyday living of life made them see it for what it really was. The passion died in them.

It was never true love in the first place it might be said here. That's the only way it can disappear. But in true twin flame relationships it can just seem to disappear, but only hide away for even a very long time. It can even appear to be a hostile split. This actually occurs because one or both partners feel 'unloved' or let down. They feel alone. Fear drives their hostility. The more passion and connection in your twin flame relationship — the more painful and emotionally hurtful will be the split. There can be words spoken and actions done against each other that later bring the tears of regret.

It is for this reason — the painful split that others see as the end of love — that the reunion and the restoration of love is your destiny. If you know you are twin flames then it can't be any other way. The hurtful split was because of the fear of lost love. The fears made it worse for both. They feared they had lost part of themselves — which of course was true as the other partner was their other half.

But if it was truly love in the first place — even in non twin flame relationships — then the love will resurface at a later date. Love can't die. It can only be hidden and it's all an illusion. If it appears to be extinguished then it can still come back with a burning fire. It just needs to be reignited. That can, most times, be a bigger fire and passion than previously.

The cause of the disappearance of love in the lives of humans can be said to be the way personalities get changed by greed and the quest for power. Some people continue on with this life quest and never see how they changed or recognise those they loved and left behind. Their trauma healing will be left for their next lifetimes.

153

Love is an energy. The most powerful energy in creation! There is only love. It is not outside of you for you to seek. It's inside you and has been there forever. You can't lose it and it can't disappear. Anything can seem to disappear but that's because of what we believe our world is. If you change your beliefs, you change your life.

The following excerpt is a love story that makes this human behaviour stand out as not even natural. You can't leave behind your true love and your true nature.

"This story is about a man who suffered a head injury and lost the last 11 years of his life. The memories were gone. Before that 11 years he was in a twin flame true love relationship with his wife and they had two beautiful children. Life was wonderful and he was a beautifully natured man. But, unfortunately in his career promotions to a high level he became bitter, strictly unwavering and unliked in his business life. It carried over into his home relationships. He was admired for his work in business but his colleagues and those working for him did not like him. One of his children became injured and needed special care. His marriage broke down because he could not put enough of himself into the love and care of his family. He had no time for that. He was an important man in his business and a workaholic by then. He then went into having an affair with someone he worked with. His wife was devastated and despaired. They broke up and divorced.

Now, the telling thing here is that when he woke up from surgery on his brain after the head injury, he had lost his memories — he only remembered who he had been 11 years ago. He remembered a loving relationship with his family and his utter devotion to his wife. They still saw each other all along and worked together. But were cold to each other. The setting worked for them both in their new life. But ... he was back in his old life. He had no clue as to why they were not together anymore. His memories of back then crowded into his brain. He relived the moments of love. He could not understand why his family were no longer together. He couldn't even fathom where his children had gone to because they were grown up now.

He also once again became very liked by all his colleagues as his nature had reverted back to how it was before his head injury, his memory loss and his promotion. He did not lord it over those working for him anymore but reorganised the work environment to be fair and helpful to others.

All he now wanted was his family back and most importantly, his wife back. His memories of why they broke up had been wiped out."

This story demonstrates what happens to humans and why their lives fall apart. With the huge amount of bad memories gone, this love story also shows how leaving past traumas behind by healing them and only believing in the positive parts of our lives will enhance all relationships.

It also shows unless we change and become like little children again and lose all the bad traits we learnt as adults such as the power trips, judgements and fears — then we can't continue to relate to others in the long term.

~~~

My Love Knows No Bounds

...

I Love You To Infinity

...

CHAPTER 11

THE HEALING JOURNEY

The healing journey will bring up many challenges. There will be chaos, twin flame running, feeling ill, suffering, obsessive thoughts, arguments, disruption, purging, bad timing and missed opportunities along the way.

All these things, most of the time, serve to make the twin flames feel a lot of pain and a huge feeling of being let down. These are just illusions but they are so very powerful and can take over your life and affect your decision making.

Before you can complete the actual reunion meeting and be one again you must first heal everything. You need to sit down and go through all the past mistakes you perceive to have contributed to your split. All the mistakes following on from this during the separation that kept you apart for a long time. When you see each mistake — write it down in your journal book. Then go through it and dissect it and see if it is still real for you. Is it still your reality? Would you now make completely different decisions? Are you in a better place now? Are all your decisions made with love now? If you can see that you have

159

learnt from it and it is no longer who you are, then you can go forward and you have healed it.

Make sure your healing journey is extensive and you have not left anything from your past hidden deeply where you can't see it in the now. This will ruin your reunion.

When I reunite with my flame it will also be a healing for a whole family. Not just 'our own' family together but for his family. They were a family of five. There was a lot of pain, arguments and splits within this family. The parents argued continuously and had more than one split in their lifetime together. They are together now in the next life but only they can know if they were ever 'twin flames'. They were certainly connected. The three children all had splits in their relationships that were all completely different.

We were, all three couples, being together in the same era with our relationships and marriages. We spent a lot of time together as couples except for the sister who was somehow unliked because of her behaviours. All three unions resulted in painful splits for very different reasons. At the present time on Earth only one couple of these three has the chance to reunite. This is because only that one couple from the group has a genuine Twin Flame incarnation. Also because of those three couples, two have lost their mate to the next life already. But one couple remains and they will reunite.

1. First, there is the sister who had what appeared to be a whirlwind and very connected love affair then marriage. They looked so connected and well matched to everyone outside their joining. But she

already had major problems with personality and past karma. She eventually suffered her own negative energies on to him relentlessly. Eventually he left her and she was devastated and also suffered a lifelong chronic painful disease. She simply could not see that she instigated the split. She died still being resentful. I do not see any twin flame relationship here. It is a soul mate connection that did not workout in this lifetime. They would still have both learnt important lessons from this relationship and even if she appears to have continued on with anger and resentment she will have the chance to change her life in her next incarnation.

2. Then the older brother had a lasting love relationship. They seemed very connected but he left her by dying suddenly and leaving this lifetime far earlier than anyone would have expected. Their relationship, all along, had been tumultuous and packed with chaos. It was still a true love. Although she went into another relationship later that was actually calmer and she found some kind of peace — she was forever devoted to this first love. She was so traumatised by his passing and the way of it that she will never love another in the same way in this lifetime. To this day she has never stopped loving him and wanting that relationship back again. She keeps the photos close to her.

3. There is also the younger son. Our own relationship. We are Twin Flames and have been

through the painful devastating split. We met so very young (16). Our connection was real and, we thought, complete. Now that I am aware, I will be bringing this true flame back into reunion with me. It's been a long process seemingly to me. But somehow I have healed many issues from the past that resulted in illness for me. I am more than ready, more than awakened and I am actively seeking now. Our reunion will seal the healing of many. Whole families will reunite.

This can be the case for many reunions. Any pain or split in relationships always affects many more people than just the two. When the reunion comes into being many other people are also healed. As I have awoken — he shall also wake up. As I have chosen this in the Now – and I create it by my Beliefs – he will also wake up in the Now.

Don't Think You Are Leaving

The Change and the Turning is not about leaving anyone or any current life. It's about 'Going To' someone and a new reignited life. It's about 'Going Home'.

It's not actually a new life but a new version of your previous life together. You will be new versions of who you were then. With all your learning and all your understanding now of who you are and who you are to each other.

Don't ever think of your life changes as losing anything or leaving anyone behind. Your focus will be on going to a burning flame that welcomes you with love. Your life is changing before your very eyes. Seek out the changes every day now.

If you are currently in a secondary relationship then if it's appropriate for your situation please make sure to leave that partner in a good place. For instance, if it means a split up of property etc, then it would be beneficial for your soul's journey to make sure this partner you are leaving has a life to go to and a good place to live. If they are open to it then you can even be involved in helping them get used to the breaking of this relationship.

This also means living two lives virtually. It is a major challenge that contributes to our reunion and advice given to those who are planning their own reunion. The closer I felt to my flame reunion — the more sour and distant my current relationship began to feel. But, if you are in a current relationship that is no longer working then you must live by allowing that person unconditional love and compassion. You will be leaving this person but there must be no animosity. This will bring about your reunion in a much faster way filled with love.

It seems like living two lives temporarily because you must put into your current relationship on a daily basis the peace and compassion that facilitates your coming change. While at the same time you are working on and planning your twin flame reunion. But you will become more and more distant to your current life as you move into the reunion life.

~~~

I Hope that in Return

...

*I Have Saved The
Best of Me
For You*

...

For you

...

CHAPTER 12

REUNION/REINVENTION

The eventual and inevitable reunion of the Twin Flames is a wonder of human existence. Using the word of 'reinvention' here also means that although they have retained their memories of joy and beauty from their past — they also must let go of any negative things they went through while parted.

Healing past traumas means in past lifetimes as well as any during their splitting time together. Therefore now they are back together in their reunion they also are reinventing their lives together to go forward in love and positivity. This love can only survive onwards when they are both healed. This reunion life together must essentially be a reinvention as well as accessing your past and eternal love for each other. This is because your ongoing life and love together is after the split and the healing — therefore it must contain both memories and new life.

Remember that you may not be reunited with your twin flame in this lifetime. The connection may miss for a number of reasons. The main one being that one or both flames do not wake up. They may miss the fact that they are part of a joining. It would be rare that neither wakes up and it would almost make it true that they are not twin flames at all. But it's also possible that after their initial joining in life that they both remain asleep and get taken in by the illusions of physical human life. But they will still be joined and the circle mended even after they have passed from this current lifetime. It's inevitable — it can't ever not happen as the two have always been one.

Equally, a twin flame may imagine they have cut cords to their mate after the break and the turning because they think they are protecting themselves from further hurt. The cords remain and are not cut in these situations. Their twin flame will just have to remain patient and forgiving and await the time that they feel the energies and return the forever connected love back to the waiting one.

Those of us who are aware of the flame connection do not give up our passions as we get older. In fact, the flame will burn even hotter and brighter the more we realise the connection and turn back towards our flame. We won't give up till our last breath on Earth.

Some people are obsessive and mistaken about their connections. There are clear signs of a Twin Flame soul connection. Some people get blinded by illusional obsession and the connection they imagine is there. But it is just not there. It's not really that common to have Twin Flame souls here on Earth. At one time in the past there may have only been as many as a few hundred Twin Flame relationships here on Earth at any one time. It is far more prevalent right now. Many souls are choosing to incarnate as

166

twins now for the purpose of evolving and also to participate in the healing of the Earth with other souls. So please realise that you are participating in a worldwide phenomenon of healing. The Earth is hurting at this present time (21st century) and you have chosen to be here right now. The present chaos, pandemics and wars can only be healed with the love contributed to by many evolved souls.

Twin Flames add their energies to this Earth healing. It can be said that many twin flame relationships are here in this lifetime for that very purpose of contributing.

How to work towards your reunion

It is important to know how to facilitate a reunion sooner rather than later and this chapter will deal with that fact.

First you must know and evaluate where you both are right now after first establishing if you really are part of a Twin Flame relationship in this lifetime. Once that is established you need to look back to see what stage you are at — read through the eight stages.

Believe that it is truly hard, once you have awakened, to stay calm and accept your life as it is before the reunion takes place. But the reunion may not occur if you don't learn this. It is actually simple, but hard to know, that you only have to 'Let Go'. You are clinging to fear and you can't see how to let go.

It can help to have a daily diary to write in. You can help yourself by writing daily what you have learned and how you intend your reunion to take place. An 'Intention' diary helps to bring about changes. If your mind creates intentions then the universal field will listen and bring about those changes and manifest them in the physical world. You can include photos or images that illustrate your intentions. The more you do this the closer the reality gets to you.

Symbolism and Creating

When you are working towards the Reunion with your Flame you also need to work with symbolism and outward signs. It's similar to daily affirmations when you practice symbolism. This means removing all visible signs of any current relationship that you have now committed to ending. Take away photos, albums, jewellery and gifts given to you by this second or other person. Wear items previously given to you by your Twin Flame, particularly jewellery if you still have anything at all. The energy of wearing items from your Twin Flame will enter through your skin into your own energy. They will then be joined energies.

Have photos of your true love around your house or even just in your wallet if you don't want others to see before you are ready. Remember about creating your 'scrap book' of memories. Old photos or other photos that remind of you of places you went together can be reprinted, copied or drawn on paper.

Other events in the past were symbols of what was to come. I'm only just recognising them now. Such as when I married the second time and I had the bouquet freeze dried and framed. The first time it was

168

done the person/company who did it made errors in the preserving. They went brown and looked dead after a short time. I should have returned them and asked for a refund or a fix up job but I didn't. The bridesmaid's also went brown. How upsetting but prophesying was this incidence.

This woman who did them also used to display her work at Wedding Fairs. This was very unprofessional work. However, later down the track I found another, better company and got them redone. Well, it seems I never gave up in those days. But the symbolism of that decision was that although they were done professionally this time — something still did occur. One flower fell off the bouquet inside the frame. I now see these symbols as pointing to my real destiny. This marriage would fail.

I have now taken framed photos and this bouquet down from the walls so they are not on display anymore. Please remove all visible and symbolic signs of any current marriage or relationship from your view. From anyone else's view also. Don't display a life you no longer are in. Put it all away and bring out the signs of your reunion and your true love.

Daily Affirmations

Use your energy and thoughts daily to bring about the reunion as early as possible. I have been doing this for quite an extended time now. I never miss a day except during the time I had surgery and was ill. He still never left my thoughts even then. But I daily do certain actions that will make sure the universal field notices and brings about my wishes and desires.

The universal field is the energy of the Creator that permeates everything that exists. Many readers would have heard of 'The Law of Attraction'. That means that you attract towards you — absolutely anything that you constantly focus on. Daily actions, thoughts and affirmations will attract to you whatever they contain and whatever you create. You are creating reunion with the Flame.

Therefore definitely do 'not' focus on any relationship you are currently in that is not your Flame. Do not give it negative energy. But learn to still love all those in your life for whatever reason they are there. It will always be for an important reason. Send them all love and empathy.

Because if you still resent any relationship you are currently in, you have not moved away from fear and negativity. Staying in these energies will interfere with your path to reunion. Even if you reunite you will be leaving behind resentment and that won't make for a happy reunion or enable it to flourish.

I write a particular affirmation every single day and connect with it.

My path in life is now clear. I see the way. I will never waver from the pathway through. All of the challenges of this lifetime are clearing the way for me. It is because I worked on what was set for me and because I have now woken up.

This can be your story too. If you are reading this book then you have chosen the path to wake up. You have recognised you have a Twin Flame relationship and you are seeking your way back.

If you can just focus on the way ahead and the life you dreamed of, then each day can bring you joy and this is probably new to anyone who is a separated Twin Flame. That newness of being happy and loving your life is something to get used to again.

In our seeking of reunion, what we two (twin flames) are really seeking is to be whole again. As we chose this kind of life we are bound to return to each other like magnets.

Twin Flame lovers don't just finally meet accidentally — they are within each other all along

Destiny

If you've ever wondered about that word (destiny), then rest assured it exists for all people and all world events.

Many people feel it. Many ignore it because they fear it. It's about the pushing and the pulling energies. We are guided in life all the way through. Some people go with it and some fight it all the way. At the same time 'free will' exists and is gifted to us.

That is what makes it so hard for many to understand. How can they exist at the same time as each other? Destiny plus Free Will. We are given both. But destiny isn't set in stone. Nothing is. That's how they exist together. There is a chosen destiny but free will can change it along the way throughout your lifetime. We are never made to do anything against our will. This is absolutely never the case. But, at the same time, that destiny we chose will come with guides and angels who push or pull us to follow the energies to our chosen path.

Even so, if you are Twin Flames you are already destined to be together. So, because you made that choice before coming here then you are joined.

If you take time to look back on your own life events you can access the knowledge and the feelings of when you were strongly guided. I know for myself I felt and remember those strong pushing and pulling times. Sometimes I nearly tried to go against them but I went with them every time. Some of them I thought were taking me to a place I did not want to go to. But looking back I see they guided me into a kind of 'valley of the shadow of death' situation. But none of us learn anything if we don't go ahead and walk through these dark times and go into the valleys. We must push on with our destiny but walk 'through' and make sure we don't allow the dark to touch us. Mostly as humans we have allowed the darkness to touch us along the way. Because we remain afraid till we have learnt to accept and go with the light at all times. But we can all still get there eventually.

I personally look back to those times when I felt strong guidance (many times it felt against my own will) and when I do this I see clearly how a whole new world opened up for me from those guided choices. This happened absolutely every time.

I was even guided to give birth to a fourth child. It didn't seem like a joint decision at the time. I could have wavered from outside pressure but I stood my ground with the choice. I felt the push and pull here also. It most certainly opened up a whole new world for me that was clearly 'destiny' for many people. Our choices and decisions always affect more than just ourselves.

The Energies

These energies we feel that are guidance — they are just nudging. They will never force you into a path you don't want in your life. If you're open to the vibrations then you will feel them and you will go with the directions. If you're not open then you may miss a huge amount of cues in your life.

Many people miss their cues and guidances. A large majority of the human race is 'asleep' for most of their lives. All are given opportunities in life to wake up and see their path.

Manifestation

The art of manifestation is always at work in our lives whether we are aware of it or not. It is the reason we manifest the bad things in life and we imagine we have not actually created it. It is because while focussing on what we fear we actually manifest it into our lives unaware.

Once you learn about manifesting then that is when you harness it to create what you truly desire in life. If you have recognised your twin flame in life and you are desiring the reunion then you will now know the reunion is inevitable. You work towards it every single day. Living it and knowing it daily will bring it towards you.

For instance if you are in a relationship or marriage that you now realise is not your flame then put away all signs of this relationship. Take down and put away any photos of you as a couple or any wedding photos or memoranda. If you have in your possession photos of you and your twin flame from the past then put these around you instead. This helps to manifest your new life together.

If you are confident about manifesting then you can also add to the outcome by, for instance, starting to pack because you are leaving your current life situation. Pack away, in a suitcase, those items you intend to take with you and some of your clothes. Get ready to leave and that includes visualising the day you leave. See yourself with the last of your suitcases packed and your twin flame coming to pick you up in his/her car.

Contribute to the Reunion

You can help the reunion along once you have woken up to your relationship. There is no pushing and trying to rush the reunion.

Meditate on the energies and send light and the colour pink to your twin flame daily or as often as you like. Always use your mind to 'live' the reunion. Play it out with visions and feel the truth of it.

You can help in other ways by creating an intention scrap book. Cover an A4 exercise book that has no lines on the pages with any imaginative patterned paper you like. Within this book is where you can paste actual old photos of your flame, photos of places you have been and you can also draw images of all these memories.

Only the good memories that you would want in your new life should be in this book of visions. Although the past memories make up who we are you still will not want to bring into the now any old negative situations or visuals. Images of activities and things that represent your time together that was good and connected.

When you have completed the book and filled it to the brim, you then regularly look through it and keep alive all the images and memories that were good and that you may actually want to relive together when you have rejoined.

Do not be put off or deluded in any way by appearances. For instance, if you see your flame with another secondary partner and they seem close and it seems like you are outside everything — be assured everything is still working out on the inner planes of existence.

Sending love and energy to the other part of your soul (twin flame) will make sure that this is also sent back to you. What we send or give to others will always come back to us. The following is a short meditation to help facilitate reconnection:

1. Sit or lie down in a quiet private space that is comfortable for you.
2. Close your eyes.
3. First, take a deep breath into the heart area and then deeper into the stomach. Then allow it to release slowly out.
4. Continue this deep breathing.
5. Think now about the person you love. This will bring up the love energy within you.
6. Smile and let the warm energy of love flow through you.
7. Send the words "I love you". Whisper the words out loud and send the warm golden feeling inside you to the person.

8. Continue this for as long as you would like.
9. Take time to come back to yourself.
10. Take another deep breath and cross both hands over your heart and breath this love energy into yourself.
11. Allow time to feel the love that you sent to your flame coming back to you.

For faster manifesting of your destiny and desires practise one of these meditations daily. Use any other meditations on Forgiveness and Healing the Past you find on YouTube or in books for the speed up and for helping to release your twin flame from any current relationships that may be blocking your reunion. Your thought system and energies you send can also dissolve the blockages.

Speed Up The Reunion

You can help to speed up the reunion in a number of ways. A few actions to consider are:

1. Write a letter to your flame (remind them of your connection).
2. Let go of the past (do this with intention).
3. Become aware of whatever is blocking your reunion.
4. Learn how to clear those blockages.
5. Practice forgiveness daily.
6. Feel and sense the presence of your twin flame with you.
7. Pack all your personal items leaving out those not connected to your twin flame. Get ready to leave.

Speak Your Destiny

You need to learn to speak your own destiny. At all times be aware of your words in life. Do not ever speak anything that is not love, balance and about where you are going. Learn to act and not to react. Reacting to people brings about spoken words that you cannot take back. They are still out there in the energy field harming people.

Words are powerful. They can send joy and love or they can bring people down and hurt them. This means speaking your life daily to everyone. Speak with positive energy to others.

The spoken word (out loud) is very powerful when creating from the 'power of intention'. Use your voice.

Also spend time alone speaking the truth of all you have learnt about yourself and your twin flame. Speak about the love, the connection, the synchronicities and the path you are on. That path leads you to the reunion. But if you speak against it or speak fears or of lost confidence you will be pulling down all the pathways you have built back towards each other.

Do Not Share

Once you know you are on the Twin Flame Reunion destiny please do not share this information with any close friends or relatives. This will diffuse your energy and may possibly stop the process of the reunion taking place. Other people's thoughts and energies being released about your private event in life can interfere with the flow. Their energies may reflect doubts about the authenticity of your life situation.

Remember at all times that your connection and your reunion is private. While the actual reunion will affect other people in a good way, it is still just your own business. It can be difficult to keep your burgeoning energies to yourself while still staying focussed on the path. It is worthwhile to make sure you contain the energies until the reunion takes place.

The absolute only time for sharing is after the reunion has taken place. Then you can share the love and share the joy. Of course and essentially, at first only share this knowledge and love with your Twin Flame. This contributes to your flame returning to you with love.

It's all about staying focussed on your true goal in life. It's not easy to keep all this restless energy to yourself but the rewards from keeping to this will be amazing.

Don't try hard to forget things and imagine you are letting the past go. The past is there for a reason. Just focus on the memories you want to remember. Those sweet memories that lift you up and allow you to work towards your reunion.

Belief Systems

Our beliefs play the most important role in our lives, our welfare, our wealth and our health. This is in absolutely everything about us.

So take a good look at your own belief system. Look at your self-talk and who and what you think you are. There is far more to this than most people will know. So once you've decided and actually 'know' that you are part of a Twin Flame relationship that's when you start to 'believe' yourself.

Change the way you see your world. Do this daily. Be there in the place you see yourself in for a reunion with your flame.

Believe it   Know it   Feel it   Be it

When things look and feel like they are falling apart — stop. Don't give in to appearances. Rise above it all. Your reunion is taking place. The whole time you are working towards it and you think it isn't here yet — well, all that time it is already done. What is destined is always already done.

Don't add fear thoughts to your creation. The law of attraction means that what you think is what you get. Accept that your wishes have been done already and they become attracted to you and appear in your life.

Daily, please spare part of your time to feeling and experiencing the actual reunion. That time will be electrifying and filled with passion. So accessing those feelings and events to live through them in the now will put you on that path of the law of attraction. It will go towards your creation and fulfilling of your wildest dreams.

Straight after I started to do this seeing and feeling the events, I had a very real dream about my flame. That had virtually not occurred during our time apart that I recall. It was vivid and real.

I was there. We were together again and it was real. It was not in any dream-like place but a real house that I know and he inhabits. We hugged and we merged. This was to be my event (the dream) that spurred on the reunion.

This dreaming is part of the feeling and sensing of your twin flame's presence. Feel that twin beside you many times daily whatever you are doing or wherever you are. Imagine you are taking their hand in yours. All these 'power of intention' actions bring your flame closer to you and enable them to feel the energy you have created.

A daily feeling of happiness and not feeling any pressure to bring about the reunion will match you to the outer world and bring about the matching of the twin flames on the physical level of life.

If you're feeling unhappy with your present situation in life and the lack of knowing when your twin flame reunion will occur — then know this — things can change very rapidly. Change can be imminent and happen faster than you could possibly allow yourself to believe.

Also take time to nurture and care for yourself because this time waiting for the reunion can be very tiring. Rest when you can. Also twin flames who have been parted for long years may both eventually suffer chronic diseases of one kind or another. Their distress at the parting and the longing to be together again can trigger illness. Many times twin flames suffer from matching health issues. This is very common actually.

Take note if this has happened in your own situation. This occurred for me and my flame. I didn't notice at first then it became obvious. This happened years apart so it was not until I got the same chronic situation and surgery that I then saw it.

Leave Nothing Behind

You will need to leave any current life and leave nothing behind. Hard as it may be, you must be very focussed on leaving and only taking those items that relate to you or your flame.

Take nothing of any previous relationship with you. No photos, no jewellery or gifts given to you and no items or furniture that you shared with another person. You will also need to be selective even with clothes you own now.

It will also be a hard decision to realise you cannot live together in any house or property with your flame if they had lived there with any other partner. That energy will be left behind to sabotage your reunion and your love passion. If there is not a real choice here due to finances then you can clear the premises out, paint all the walls, get new bedding and burn a sage smudge stick. Buy furniture you have chosen together.

Be very critical in your assessment of what you take with you. Never take anything that connects you with any relationships that came between you and your flame.

Once Upon A Time

In My Wildest Fantastic Dreams

I would never have dreamed of us ever parting

Come home now

Free yourself to be with me

Forevermore

I wish we'd just had a true love lifetime together
with no split

BUT …

Clearly we weren't ready or evolved enough
We needed the lessons and the reunion
We chose it all – Our pact
Reunion and Fire is so very Sweet
Sweeter for the split and rejoining

~~~

Touch your lips to mine

And hold me in your arms

…

We will return in every
Lifetime

…

CHAPTER 13

LOVE HEALS

The Twin Flame connection meaning represents healing and atonement. That is the true purpose and souls agree to this kind of incarnation for the purpose of healing. That is, healing of the self and healing of the Earth Mother.

Some souls split their energies into Twin Flames for the purpose of essential work here on Earth. They spend their lives together in work such as research, spiritual guidance or Earth conservation. Some Twin Flames are here to work on a higher purpose for all.

Other twin flames are here for a major romantic relationship that will bring all the pain of the split, running and chasing. These people are here for their own soul healing and learning but it will also span out to include others in the healing such as those close to them and family members.

Through this incarnation the soul who splits into two has a destiny of healing in this lifetime. There are many past traumas for the majority of souls. Various lifetimes have hurt them and made them unaware of love for themselves and forgiveness for themselves. First love and forgive yourself before attempting to do this towards others. You simply cannot love or forgive others unless you first do it for yourself. You have not learned how to express this to others if not for yourself first and foremost. This is the great learning that many cannot understand. Loving yourself is not being selfish. It is the opposite. You can't learn unconditional love and oneness if you have not included yourself first.

Many souls practice 'self loathing'. This means they are retaining negative emotions and energies within themselves and towards themselves. They are lost in the darkness of depression and fear. This is the case for many people right now as there is a lot of chaos in the world and potential dangers and fears.

Those of us who access the love are bound to share it and help to heal those around us. This dark negativity directed within is harmful and self limiting. They are throwing daggers into their own hearts. When you have this kind of negative emotion towards yourself — and a lot of the time it is so deeply hidden that it can't even be seen — then it darkens and damages any kind of emotion or energy that you send out to others and the world.

In this life, nothing can be owned but at the end when the reunion has taken place only love remains forever. This is all that we seek in our learning experience of Twin Flames. When we are in the seeking stage after the running and chasing stages — what we are seeking is unconditional love. We are essentially seeking ourselves. There is nothing else.

Love never hurts others but fulfils the requirements of the universe. So, on your journey back to reuniting, any other partners involved temporarily should never be hurt. If you don't direct arrows or hurts towards them to rid yourself of them they will simply fade away naturally if your twin flame relationship is real. Yes, so sometimes when you are ready to reunite with your flame they will be in a secondary relationship still. They will perhaps still be feeling the hurt of your split. They may cling to this other relationship but be assured that it will still dissolve.

One of the main reasons we know these other relationships will dissolve is the inevitability of the twin flame incarnation's destiny. So there is never a reason to push or stress over this outcome. Accept and know that you are supported and guided.

Alone we are one drop in the ocean — but together we are united as the whole ocean. Think of life as the ebb and flow of the ocean. We are never stagnant. When you free your mind in the rejoining of the flame circle you free your body also. Many illnesses may spontaneously disappear and you may regenerate to a large degree. This enables you to enjoy the rest of your lives together and be joined once again.

The healing power of love is not to be thought of lightly. It is the ultimate reason for this existence on the human level. It is why we come here.

Love heals absolutely everything. From wars, racism, discrimination, sexism, hatred and bullying — these will drift away from our planet. Also we see the way many humans are degrading the very earth and oceans we live with and depend on for sustenance. Before that healing is complete the world will experience chaos, war and disease.

This is what we are going through right now in 2021.

There is beauty beyond understanding in this world. Take the time to see and feel this beauty. Stop rushing and living only on the surface each day. This is how you can stop the noise and confusion in your daily life and then you will see not only the detail, the quiet and the beauty but you will see your own destiny.

~~~

Never Let Me Go

...

*Now That I Have
Found You Again*

...

I Will Never Let Go Again

About the Author

Coral Cross started her education in the writing field at art school, studying art history and writing short stories. Her intention was always to publish some day. But in the mean time she studied photography, graphic design and illustration. She then worked for many years in the editorial section of magazines and newspapers and eventually as an advertising designer. Coral Cross has worked in the healing and spiritual areas for many years. She is qualified in Kahuna Massage/Healing, Bodywork, and Pranic (energy) Healing.

She has used the base of this healing education and qualifications to go deep and evolve spiritually to the point where she has developed a way to access intuitive information for healing and writing.

She has self published two other books dealing with healing chronic pain and illness which you can find at www.choose-to-heal.com.au

These two books will be also published as paperbacks in the coming months. Entitled 'Surviving Fibromyalgia' and 'Healing Practices'.